INSPIRATIONAL LEADERSHIP

Books by Lance Secretan

Managerial Moxie: The 8 Proven Steps to Empowering Employees and
Supercharging Your Company
The Masterclass: Modern Fables for Working and Living
The Way of the Tiger: Gentle Wisdom for Turbulent Times
Living the Moment: A Sacred Journey
Reclaiming Higher Ground: Creating Organizations that Inspire the Soul
Spirit@Work Cards: Bringing Spirit and Values to Work

CDs by Lance Secretan

Reclaiming Higher Ground: Creating Organizations that Inspire the Soul
Inspirational Leadership: Destiny, Calling and Cause
The Keys to the Castle: The Magic of Higher Ground Leadership
The New Story of Leadership: Reclaiming Higher Ground
Values-Centered Leadership: A Model for Work and Life

Videos by Lance Secretan

Values-Centered Leadership: A Model for Work and Life
Reclaiming Higher Ground: Organizations that Inspire the Soul
Inspirational Leadership: Destiny, Calling and Cause
The Keys to the Castle: The Magic of Higher Ground Leadership

If you would like to contact the author to order his books, videos, or CDs, please do
so at the following address:

Dr. Lance H. K. Secretan
The Secretan Center Inc.
R.R. #2
Alton, Ontario
L0N 1A0 CANADA

Lance Secretan's Web Site

E-mail: info@secretan.com
Web: www.secretan.com

For public speaking engagements, please contact:

W. Colston Leigh Inc. Advisory Services LLC.
1065 US Hwy 22
Bridgewater, NJ 08807
Phone: 908.253.8600
Fax 908.253.8601
Web: http://www.Leighbureau.com
E-mail: info@Leighbureau.com

INSPIRATIONAL LEADERSHIP

Destiny, Calling and Cause

LANCE H. K. SECRETAN

National Library of Canada Cataloguing in Publication

Secretan, Lance H. K.
    Inspirational leadership : destiny, calling and cause / Lance H.K. Secretan

Includes bibliographical references.
ISBN 0-9694561-9-0

    1. Leadership.   2. Leadership--Moral and ethical aspects.
3. Organizational effectiveness.   I. Title.

HD57.7.S43 2003   658.4'092   C2003-902948-4

The Secretan Center Inc.

Printed in Canada

Table of Contents

LANCE SECRETAN'S:

Destiny:

*To help create a more sustainable
and loving planet*

Personal Cause:

*To inspire others to honor
the sacredness in all relationships*

Corporate Cause:

*To change the world
by reawakening spirit and values
in the workplace*

Calling:

*To lead and serve through my writing,
teaching and speaking*

Acknowledgments

An old Zen saying tells us that "the teacher teaches the lessons he most needs to learn." For the last forty years, I have been a student of leadership. My greatest teacher, apart from formal studies and some amazing mentors, has been practice. As a CEO of several companies, I have been able to conduct experiments in living laboratories. As a public speaker, I address some 200,000 people every year — audiences are wonderful critics of radical theories! As a consultant, I find my clients quick to sort out the wheat from the chaff, too. As for being a writer, book sales are a meticulous measure of whether concepts hit the mark or not. So I use every avenue I can to experiment, teach, and learn. I thank my clients, readers, audiences, colleagues and critics for being so friendly, forgiving, honest, insightful, generous, spirited and loving. I thank my clients, too, for their inspiration — it is a gift to the heart to see so many leaders inspiring others and changing the world for the better — especially when there is so much dismal data about dispirited people at work. Thank you for the privilege of sharing in your inspirational journeys, and allowing me to write about you and the spirited, values-centered path you are charting. Ernest Hemingway said, "My aim is to put down on paper what I see and what I feel in the best and simplest way." I have tried to do the same.

The Inspirational Leaders we interviewed for this book were patient, forthright, and brilliantly insightful — their stories enhanced our experience and, we hope, the quality of the concepts we are trying to convey.

My team at the Secretan Center is my sanctuary and my inspiration. I am especially grateful to Tammy Hunt-Sullivan (Manager of WOW), Susan Neath (Director of Teaching Tools), Linda Michon (Director of Synergy), and John Pollock (Director of Unlimited Possibilities) for being living examples of the concepts of leadership and followership this book describes. And we cannot overlook our Wonder Dog, Spirit (Director of Unconditional Love), who brings her own extraordinary presence to our team.

Our worldwide team of Secretan Associates has been a marvelous source of ideas, criticism, insights, wisdom, experience, editorial, and research support. They include Carole Alphonso, Brenda Anderson, Chris Angus, Jacquie Brandt, Lisa Brock, Moe Bruce, Erin Caldwell, Colin

Campbell, Mike Carter, Leonore Clauss, Deborah Clifford, Lianne Collins, Sunny Daljit, Tina DeSalvo, David Doey, Linda Foss, Julie Francisco, Delayne Giardini, Aileen Gibb, Helen Goldstein, Joyce Gwilliam, Betty Healey, Diane Hoover, Dawn Joy, Carol Kaye, Karyn Klapecki, Andi Lothian, Georgia Lucas, Maureen McCarthy, Craig McDowall, Phil Mittertreiner, Aisling Monahan, Mark Moreau, Helen Morley, Susan Nind, Patrick O'Sullivan, Colodia Owens, Ruben Palechiz, Rebecca Parkes, John Pollock, Steve Robinson, Tricia Secretan, Sid Segal, Zorina Swallow, Doug Upchurch, Ruth Webber and Catherine Wood.

Catherine Wood provided invaluable sources of research and a loving and intelligent contribution that could only have come from a heart that is in the same space as mine. She worked closely with our many clients who are practicing Inspirational Leadership® and brilliantly captured the essence of their wonderful work. Another Associate, Susan Nind, gave an unflinching but loving feedback during the writing of the manuscript.

The team at Leigh Bureau has been a constant source of support, insight, and inspiration, particularly Ron Szymanski and Tom Neilssen, as well as Ginger Albright, Mike Humphrey, Larry Leson, Karen Leodice, Anne Pace, Danny Stern, Les Tuerk, Robin Wolfson, and the late, and greatly missed, Fern Weber.

Thanks to Diane Spivak, who wrestled nobly with my unruly prose in early drafts, thus coaxing it into greater coherence.

My wife, Tricia (Moccasin Walker), is a continuing source of inspiration for everything I do in life. She is magic, she nurtures my soul, and she makes my life complete. This book contains much of her wisdom and practical input and is a product of our love. She is my Inspirational Leader.

Meditation of an Inspirational Leader

*As we are gathered together as colleagues,
let us be truly together — as one.*

(Silence — reflect for a moment)
Let us pay attention to our breathing.
(Silence)
Let us center in our bodies and our minds.
(Silence)
Let us calm our bodies and our minds.
(Silence)
Let us go within.
(Silence)
Let us put a half-smile on our faces and cause it to
flow to every corner of our beings.
(Silence)
Let us reflect on The Source of each of us,
our colleagues, and everything in the Universe.
(Silence)
From The Source, let us fill our hearts with love and compassion —
towards each other and all living things.
(Silence)
Let us remember that we are all living beings, brothers and sisters,
nourished by the same Source of life.
(Silence)
Let us resolve to cease being a cause of suffering to
each other at work and throughout life.
(Silence)
Let us resolve to live and work in a way that does not
harm our Planet — and instead heals it.
(Silence)
Let us resolve to live and work in a way that harms
no other living beings — and instead supports them.
(Silence)
With humility, and the recognition of the sacredness of life,
let us pray for and practice loving kindness.
(Silence)
Let us share sacred space together on Higher Ground.

INTRODUCTION

People often ask me to define the soul. I cannot do it. So many others have also tried. But this I know: the soul is bigger than any single corporation, government, community, family, healthcare facility, law enforcement, religious or learning institution. No single organization is big enough for the soul. Of one thing we can be sure: our soul is infinite and part of the largest universe we can imagine — and then some.

Goodbye Old Story. Hello New Story.

A leader who does not inspire is like a river without water.

Every follower yearns to be inspired by his or her leader. Indeed every person yearns to be inspired by every other person. When we fail to do so, we diminish each other and sadden our souls. Thus, the role of the leader is to inspire.

What compelled followers to dedicate themselves with such passion to the visions of Jefferson, Washington, Christ, Buddha, Gandhi, Confucius, Martin Luther King Jr., Mother Teresa, and Nelson Mandela? They were inspired, not motivated. We know that Martin Luther King did not say, "I have a strategic plan!" And Mother Teresa did not have a quality program — she didn't need one. As we unravel the mysteries of these subtle but significant nuances in leadership style, we find that inspiration underpinned the philosophy of every great leader.

Profits are up but people are down. We live in paradoxical times. Economic output soars while corporations restructure and reinvent themselves in order to meet the pressures of globalization and competition. Wall Street booms as 625,000 people lose their jobs. Even as employees are being asked to do more with less, the ratio of CEO pay to that of the average worker has gone from 27:1 in 1973 to 48:1 in 1998. The social contract ("I will commit my working life to the firm if the firm guarantees to provide me with secure employment until I retire"), so long taken for granted, has been shattered, along with the dreams of many, giving rise to a new class of independent workers: independent contractors as "lone eagles" and employees as "free agents." Corporations have never done so well, but global competition is squeezing margins and putting a lid on prices. It is like a day when the sun is out, but it is raining.

There is a growing sense of anxious anticipation in the modern workplace, of impending change: the shadow of apprehension, disenchantment, and betrayal conflicts with the light of hope, opportunity, and new beginnings. These are confusing times. They are exciting times.

3

From Institutional to Inspirational Thinking

Traveling as much as I do, delays inevitably occur and the reactions of passengers vary. Some are charming and philosophical, while others take their rage out on harassed airline employees. I often look at those passengers who harangue the airline employees who are struggling to deal with the complexities of travel and I wonder, "Do you really think that you will achieve your goals with your hostile, aggressive, insulting, and demeaning behavior?" How did we forget the old adage that more flies are caught with honey than with vinegar? Where did we learn the myth that we can get our way more effectively with petulance or through aggression than with love? In our hearts we know that we will achieve more by serving others than by venting our anger. Try this experiment: next time you find yourself in an exasperating and frustrating situation in an airport, ask the flight attendant, "Is there anything I can do to make your day go a little more smoothly?" Then watch the frustration melt and the employee's helpfulness grow. This is the magic of service.

> **The wealth of a soul is measured by how much it can feel; its poverty by how little.**
> WILLIAM ROUNSEVILLE ALGER

After working with the American Heart Association on a couple of assignments, Tina Zarifes, AHA Regional Director in Los Angeles, asked me how to persuade Larry King to become the honorary chair of the annual Griffith Park Heart Walk in Los Angeles. I suggested to her that she avoid the usual approach of building a water-tight case, with a snappy proposal, to "sell" him on why he should become the honorary chair of the walk. Instead, I suggested that she ask him some questions, such as, "What are you looking for when you become involved with charities or sponsorships? What are you trying to achieve in your life? How can the American Heart Association help you to achieve some of your life's goals? How can I serve you through the AHA?" She called me a few days later to let me know she had used this approach and Larry King had agreed to become the chairperson of the Los Angeles AHA Griffith Park Heart Walk.

> **We don't see things as they are, we see things as we are.**
> ANAÏS NIN

The difference between old story leadership and new story leadership is similar to the difference between order and chaos. Old story leaders search for order by imposing systemwide motivation; Inspirational Leaders, new story leaders, accept and encourage chaos through one-soul-at-a-time inspiration. Old story leaders create processes that are designed to reinforce systemwide behavior. They prefer to control by creating order, establishing rules, and defining and achieving goals and outcomes. The Inspirational Leader trusts the genius of the spirit.

Here is another way to look at the contrast: old story leaders are Newtonian thinkers; Inspirational Leaders are quantum thinkers. On the one hand, the laws of dynamics govern Newtonian thinking. The laws of dynamics predict that everything in the Universe will implode into a cold and empty void. On the other hand, quantum physics describes a Universe that is constantly reinventing and adapting itself.

Newtonian thinking is by nature pessimistic and negative; quantum thinking is optimistic and hopeful. Old story leaders expect the world, and consequently their organizations, to run down, like the cosmic clock, at some point in the future. This has implications for the way that they interact with people. A pessimistic old story leader seeks control over others in order to limit the implosion. Some old story leaders are more optimistic — they hope that the breakdown can be held off, if only for a short time. Thus, old story leaders are both short-term thinkers and pessimists in the long term. They believe they can influence the short-term outcomes of the organization, but that in the long run it will die, together with all of its parts — the people within.

> **People are voting for the artist and not the painting.**
>
> WARREN BUFFETT

The energy of organizations differs — some are Newtonian and some are quantum, sometimes they are one or the other, sometimes they are both at the same time, and sometimes they are both in different parts of the system. Thus, one division can feel quite different from another, the organization can feel different when leaders change, and they can feel as though they are about to implode or to expand.

We often talk about organizations as if they were animated — what social scientists call anthropomorphism — ascribing human characteristics to what is not human. Organizations do not exist — they are legal constructs. It is the souls within them that exist. Newtonian old story leaders often can't see the individual, instead viewing the organization as a complete machine that can be influenced through "group" motivation, while quantum leaders see the quanta that are ever changing and morphing into the system.

Organizations cannot inspire, only people can, but it is possible to create an inspiring organization. There is just one way to do this: by inspiring people, one soul at a time. There is no other way.

We are saying goodbye to the old story and hello to the new story...
Goodbye fear and control;
Hello heart and soul.

Who Is a Leader?

Who isn't a leader? Mothers, brothers, sisters, friends, and strangers are all called upon at different times to lead. So are teachers, principals and students; taxi drivers, bus drivers, and truck drivers; nurses, doctors, and clinicians; law enforcement officers, attorneys, defendants, and plaintiffs; salespeople and customers; actors, musicians, poets and artists; athletes, coaches, sports administrators, and referees; politicians, ministers, and constituents. Who of us during some point in our day is not called upon to display leadership skills? When I refer to leaders in *Inspirational Leadership,* I mean to include everyone — especially CEOs, presidents, senior executives, managers — but all of the rest of us, too.

Leaders and Parceners

When we think of leaders, we also think of followers. The word *follower* carries with it a certain "upstairs, downstairs" connotation, a sense of hierarchy that is unhelpful to discussions that might lead to enlightened leadership. The term *parcener* (pronounced pars·ner) is derived from a French word, which in law means a person who shares jointly with others in an inheritance. As leaders and followers, which are roles we all play interchangeably throughout each day of our lives, we share an inheritance to serve and inspire each other — we are partners. In turn, we pass on this inheritance in the form of a legacy. We are forever shifting between our roles as leaders and followers. An orchestra provides a useful metaphor for the interdependent nature of leadership. Like the first violinist in a great orchestra, we must follow and lead at the same time. Sometimes, followers must switch to a leadership role, and leaders must willingly follow. We are leaders and followers at different times, sometimes even during the same conversations or activities. The one-dimensional stereotype of leaders and followers that occurs in so much of our literature and our leadership practice is not only out of date, it needs new language. Throughout this book, therefore, we will substitute *parcener* as the term for follower.

The Powerful Energies of Change

Seismic changes are reshaping the landscape of work.

The first change is the growth in public awareness, self-responsibility, and accountability. Patients know more about their own health today than their physicians did two decades ago; they often know more than their specialist medical advisors. When *Fortune* magazine ran a cover article about prostate cancer, it was Andy Grove, chairman of Intel Corp., not cancer specialists, who made the cover. Inside were eleven pages describing Grove's illness, his research, his research techniques, and how he made his treatment decisions. For additional insights reporters turned to other prostate cancer victims, including Norman Schwarzkopf and Michael Milken.[1]

We live in an age where everyone is an expert on all popular subjects, and some are experts on the arcane. Because people have experienced the fallibility of professionals and the systems in which they practice, they have concluded that it is in their best self-interests to reclaim responsibility for their own lives through self-education and advocacy. They have found a cornucopia of data in journals, popular science, and medical reports, specialist associations, radio, television, movies and theater, non-mainstream advisors, and the Internet, where a wealth of instant information is available. Our access to education and information has never been greater, and this search for, and acceptance of, personal accountability is being repeated in every facet of our lives. As a result, we are all now mini-specialists in a wide range of areas, including healthcare, education, politics, religion, the environment, and work.

The second major energy of change is the growth of "leadership fatigue." In the workplace, there has been a dramatic growth in the understanding of the dynamics and practice of leadership. Wide access into boardrooms, corporate decision-making processes, and the inner workings of organizations has begun to demystify leadership. It is no longer something that is practiced by an elite few and "done" *to* others. Increasingly, leadership is a co-created activity.

In the past, almost everyone, from tin-pot dictators to schoolyard bullies, not to mention old story CEOs and religious and political leaders, learned the technology of "power-based leadership" — a fear-based leadership that seeks to manipulate, control, and dominate followers. We know the signs and traits, we've heard the sports coaches and corporate gurus, and we've read the books and gone to the leadership seminars. We now know the language of traditional leadership when we hear it. We are sensitive to the tendency of many leaders to manipulate us for their own ends — and we resent it.

As a result, the power-driven leader now has to contend with cynical and unresponsive parceners, weary with leadership jargon and techniques. They have heard it all before — the "win-this-once-for-the-Gipper" urgings, the slogans and T-shirts, the hype of conferences, and the internal PR programs. This has made them a jaded audience for leaders. This is a sure sign that a paradigm shift is occurring. The new leadership model is based on values, service, and spirit and is set to become the central plot line of the new story of leadership.

> **Last night I asked an old wise man to tell me all the secrets of the universe. He murmured slowly in my ear, "This cannot be told, but only learned."**
>
> RUMI

The third significant change is the dramatic and universal search for greater meaning in our lives that is sweeping the world. A growing number of people are embracing the notion that we are spiritual beings with spiritual needs, not just personalities with ego needs. The old story of power-based leadership appealed to the personality. But people crave nourishment for their souls. They are asking their leaders to be aware of, and care for, their spiritual needs and to lead from the heart. Parceners are looking for leaders who will build their spiritual muscles.

The old story model of leadership, still used by many even as it expires, is based on the concept of the leader as a *warrior* and reveres icons such as Attila the Hun, Machiavelli, the Samurai warriors, and military generals such as Patton and McArthur, Napoleon Bonaparte, and the Duke of Wellington.

For example, the value of the original investment in CF&I Steel LP's Pueblo, Colorado, steel mill increased by 675% between 1993 and 1998, while employee productivity increased 78% from 1995 to June 1997. Employees were shocked and angered when management labor contract proposals included higher healthcare co-payments and deductibles and a wage offer that was still below the industry average.[2] A bitter strike lasting two years was the angry response — egos talking with egos, masks talking with masks. Such ego-based models of leadership no longer work.

The new story uses models of leadership that honor a different kind of leader: Jefferson, Buddha, Gandhi, Mother Teresa, Martin Luther King, Jr., Christ, Confucius, Lao-tzu, and Nelson Mandela. The new leader is loved not feared. The new leader inspires rather than motivates. The new leader serves his or her parceners. Parceners are the *customers* of the new leader, and new leaders strive to meet or exceed the needs of parceners.

If one advances confidently in the directions of his dreams, and endeavors to live the life which he has imagined, he will meet with a success unexpected in common hours.

HENRY DAVID THOREAU

Great leaders develop a vision so compelling that it becomes a magnet for passion — a Cause. They do not espouse cookie-cutter approaches to leadership. Nor do they repeat spiels from motivational tapes. In fact, they do not try to motivate — *they invite inspiration.* They combine visceral energy with a clear and focused vision, founded on strong spiritual beliefs and values. This combination radiates a light so bright that parceners find it irresistible. Inspirational Leaders do not need to recruit because their Cause becomes a beacon, attracting the passion of people from far and wide. Modern corporate examples abound — The Body Shop, ServiceMaster, Medtronic, W.L. Gore, Southwest Airlines, Patagonia, Whole Food Markets, and Malden Mills. The best-led organizations of our time consist of inspired individuals and teams who epitomize the new story of leadership. They are inventing the new standards of leadership that employee-customers are yearning for in the next millennium. As Pierre Teilhard de Chardin wrote, "Someday, after mastering the winds, the tides and gravity, we shall harness for God the energies of love, and then, for a second time in the history of the world, man will have discovered fire."[3]

Some of us are asleep and some of us are awake. Some of us are still clinging to the old story; but there are a growing number of us who want to write the new story. The great excitement of our times is the growing number of people who are awakening from their deep sleep, to the realization that they are experiencing an acute spiritual hunger, an inner sense of restlessness and desire for a greater sense of purpose in their lives. As a force that leads to radical change, no power in the Universe is greater than a soul that seeks to satisfy its spiritual hunger. Parceners know this. We all stand at the dawn of a new era of awakening. The greatest idea in leadership practice that will shape the next few years is the awareness that leaders must tune in to the wisdom and spirit of their parceners.

The role of the leader is to inspire. This is a book about inspiration.

FINDING THE WAY

The model of spiritual leadership proposed by this book contrasts to the theories of leadership widely practiced in modern organizations and in society. Before we look at this radically different model of leadership, we need to review our current thinking about leadership, the reasons why we sense so much discomfort with the popular models as they are practiced today, and the major forces that are converging in such a momentous way to cause us to rethink these practices.

Inspirational Leadership is divided into two parts. Part One explains the circumstances that led to our present intense hunger for a better way to lead others, for a way to inspire and ennoble them and their souls, for a way that all leaders can act toward every living and inanimate thing as sacred. History and mythology have much to say about leadership, and we will draw on this inheritance for some of our wisdom. We also have as much or more to learn from the examples of the greatest leaders that ever lived, including many contemporary ones.

Part Two explains the path to becoming an inspirational leader, which consists of a seven-step approach that has been followed by many of the greatest historical and contemporary Inspirational Leaders.

The End of Old Story Leadership Theory

We are experiencing a leadership paradox of staggering proportions: corporate leaders struggle to find ways to increase organizational effectiveness in times of wrenching change, while those they lead are disconnecting from them in growing numbers. As leaders strive harder to motivate and influence their teams, this disaffection increases.

My company researches the feelings of employees about their work. A recent "Secretan Work Enjoyment Survey" polled across Canada and the United States found that two-thirds of respondents do not trust their co-workers. More than half gain no spiritual nourishment from their work or inspiration from their physical working environments. The same number report excessive bureaucracy. One in two persons reports unhappy relationships with management, colleagues, customers, and suppliers; they lack the information necessary to do their work; and they lack pride in the way profits are earned. *Nearly half do not look forward to going to work on Monday mornings.* Remember the old joke?

> **The best proof of love is trust.**
>
> DR. JOYCE BROTHERS

Question: What's the difference between a chain gang and a corporation?

Answer: On a chain gang you get to work outside.

Why is this happening?

Perhaps the answer is that it is because we have become more committed to results than to people. One of the world's most respected management theorists wrote recently in the *Harvard Business Review,* "Organizations need to remember that their ultimate goal is performance, not employee satisfaction and morale."[4] Perhaps we have lost sight of the point: organizations are meant to serve people, not the other way around. One small indication of our commitment to results over leadership is the increasing erosion of the conventional lunch-hour in the name of productivity. More than half of all employees (55%) now take fifteen minutes or less for lunch, or skip it altogether. Insecurity created by massive layoffs, isolation, and lack of long-standing friendships at work because of workplace transience concerns researchers who believe that worker burnout may become an epidemic. Jeffrey Mayer, author of *Time Management for Dummies,* says, "Lunch time has become stress time." We must ask ourselves as leaders: Is this an inspiring leadership style? Does it serve the best interests of employees — and therefore customers as well as the broader community? How far do we wish to travel from what we have cast aside, a time when we honored time and the present moment?

What are the consequences of pursuing results at the expense of people? A sad and alarming one is the ruthless replacement of mature and wise parceners with younger ones who are paid less and are free of family responsibilities and ready to work ninety-hour weeks. At Westech Career Expos, the biggest technology job fair in America, the registration form invites attendees to check their "professional minority status," one of which is "over forty."[5] Baby boomers, all of whom are now over forty, will hardly feel inspired by leaders who affront their souls by discriminating against wisdom in this way. Remember the sergeant in *Hill Street Blues* who finished each police briefing with the words "Be careful out there"? This is good advice for those over forty in a world where reducing costs, increasing profits and boosting results are more important than people.

> **It is quite wrong to think of age as a downward slope. On the contrary, one climbs higher and higher with the advancing years, and that, too, with surprising strides. Brain-work comes as easily to the old as physical exertion to the young.**
>
> GEORGE SAND

The goals of most corporate executives have become a boring mantra: maximizing productivity and shareholder value; lowering costs; widening margins; raising quality and customer-service standards; and increasing sales and market share. Many corporate leaders believe employees need to hear these incantations over and over again and that constant repetition — in courses, speeches, and memos — will bring about increased performance. But employees have heard it all before. They have the T-shirt, they've been to the workshop, and they have tuned out. Employees doubt the authenticity of leaders who tell them they are the organization's most important asset one day, and then fire a hundred of their colleagues the next. Employees already understand the goals of management and how to achieve them. They know what is necessary to improve productivity, quality, and customer satisfaction. What they want to know is:

- Does management care?
- Is my job secure?
- How can I achieve greater meaning and fulfillment from my work?
- Am I being told the truth?
- Is this an organization with integrity?
- Are our leaders compassionate?
- Do they respect me and treat me as a spiritual being rather than just a means of production?
- Does my contribution matter?

When parceners are convinced that their leaders value these concerns through their behavior and genuine concern for their spiritual wellness, parceners will do everything it takes to help their leaders to succeed. They will do this because they will know that their leaders wish to serve parceners — as spiritual beings.

The Old Story of Leadership

Our leadership models spring from the cult of personality and celebrity that is the corporate culture of our time. Though subject to many variations and interpretations, the model that old story leaders follow consists of four steps:

1. **Develop a shared vision and mission.** Old story leaders craft a shared vision together with their leadership team — as a sort of "bonding" exercise — usually a "man thing." This results in the widely practiced ritual of forming a committee to define our dreams. When Winston Churchill observed that "a camel is a horse designed by a committee," he must have been thinking about committees whose mission statements were lame.

2. **Orchestrate the "buy-in" to the vision.** Once the vision and mission statements are created and approved by all of the "stakeholders," the old story leaders hit the road to drum up support for them. This "dog-and-pony-show," familiar to all corporate denizens, becomes the vehicle for gathering disciples — for rousing employees, unions, customers, shareholders, and suppliers, to "buy in" to the *new vision*

and *mission*. If parceners discover that the message is simply old wine in new bottles, their sense of disenchantment deepens, and they are alienated from their leaders.

3. **Develop a strategy to achieve the vision.** The next task for the old story leaders is to develop the strategic plan that will move the organization towards the (now shared) *new vision*. This entails a broad-ranging collaboration among several functions, including marketing, operations and finance, as well as human resources and information technology. The goal of this process is to ensure that everyone feels "empowered" through their contribution. The underlying theory is that if people help to design the *new vision,* they will "own" it, and if this process succeeds, it will achieve the most powerful buy-in.

4. **Motivate employees and implement the strategy.** Lastly, the old story leaders assemble the team that will implement the strategy. The job of the leaders now is to motivate the employees to achieve the strategy that will lead to the *new vision*.

This is a mechanical model based on an old concept of leadership that seeks to manipulate, control, and exploit the personality. But it ignores the one thing people yearn to nourish — their spirit.

Building Communities of Relationships

The subatomic particles that make up the book you hold in your hands give it *the appearance* of a thing, but it does not exist and therefore cannot do anything. The relationships between the author and scores of other people in his life, and all the experiences that accrued from them, generated the energy that became the author's ideas. These ideas became keystrokes in a computer and eventually electronic code; then, after passing through the wisdom and experience of many others, they were sent by technicians to a machine that put ink on paper, which came to the bindery as a result of the skills of foresters, not to mention Mother Nature. Editors, publishers, lawyers, agents, publicists, reviewers, and many others created more relationships. Eventually, "a book" was produced, but a result is not a cause. It still cannot come alive until it lives in the hearts of others who like it well enough to encourage you to first buy it, and then read it. Finally, you sit on an airplane or on a beach or in an easy chair and decide to build a relationship with all those people by reading the book. Even if you read every page from front to back (oh, I wish it were true!), the book does not exist until you take action, which means creating a relationship with someone. Until then, it still has no meaning. Nothing exists until a relationship exists.

In the same way, organizations cannot do anything, because they do not exist, either. The Japanese do not even have a word to describe "individual," the concept of the community and the family having such powerful societal sway. Only when we view our organizations for what they are — communities of relationships — can we create reality. This reality is of two kinds: material reality, which, as we learn from quantum physics, consists of the relationships between space and tiny subatomic particles, and spiritual reality, which consists of the relationships between the souls with whom we interact in the communities we call organizations.

> **The conclusion of both modern physics and deep psychology are that things are not what they seem. What we experience as normal reality — about ourselves and nature — is only the tip of an iceberg that arises out of an unfathomable abyss.**
>
> THOMAS MOORE

Strong relationships are inclusionary; that is, they seek to embrace rather than repel or exclude. Organizations, of any kind, cannot be relevant if they seek to exclude by creating hierarchies, which separate people by their status or power. For example, old story leaders still cling to such archaic notions as "employee," "boss," and "subordinate." The language of separation and exclusion marks old story thinking, where it is common to hear people described as being "in scope" or "out of scope" or pigeon-holed into caste systems with labels like "hourly" or "salaried." The soul seeks to belong, to create relationships and to be part of a community. In building great organizations we are seeking to build communities to which we contribute and from which we are nourished — a holistic, symbiotic relationship built on acceptance and permission among members that leads to more than just survival,

> **The one thing in the world, of value, is the active soul.**
>
> RALPH WALDO EMERSON

but to growth and evolution. Most importantly, it must lead to spiritual nourishment, a deep and mutual caring of the souls — of all members. This is the essence of relationships in a community.

If we continue to maintain a materialistic worldview, our picture of life will be made up only of discrete *things*, and we will tend to view people the same way. The *things* perspective results in actions that make us feel like separate, unrelated things. It results in actions that are good for me but bad for you — win-lose combinations. Sometimes this shows up in careless atti-tudes to the environment or to people. The endless re-organizations, restructurings, downsizings, refocusings, and "programs" that are the quintessential knee-jerks of the old story, thing-centered leaders in modern organizations, have gravely damaged the quality of relationships. As a con-sequence, many people feel betrayed and discarded as mere things, rather than as the "most important assets" their leaders once claimed them to be.

In July 1996, a fire roared through the Carmenet vineyards of Napa, destroying precious cabernet sauvignon, cabernet franc, and Merlot grapes. Managing director Michael Richmond, winemaker Jeffrey Baker, and three other employees hosed down the roof of the winery to prevent it from burning down. Although the winery survived, 75% of Carmenet's high-margin crop was destroyed. Two poor harvests in previous years combined with the blaze seemed to spell catastrophe. The day after the fire, Joel Peterson of the competing Ravenswood Winery called, and pledged replacement grapes to Carmenet a few hours later. The Sonoma Valley Vintners and Growers Alliance asked its 135 members to help, and offers poured in. "Even the smallest growers with only an acre called," said exec-utive director Christine Finlay. "They all thought it might have been them." Local wineries sold grapes to Carmenet, even though doing so cut into their own production of premium wines. Said Ravenswood's Peterson, "It's to my advantage to have Carmenet around. They're good people, they pro-duce good wine, and they're out in the market supporting the stuff I believe in. By selling their wine, I'm in effect selling my own."[6] That is how com-munities built on strong relationships thrive and grow. We are human spir-its sharing the same time and space, here to serve each other, not crush each other in competition for more things.

It is time for us to freshen up our perspective, from a *things* view of the world to one that sees the sacredness in relationships and communities *as well as things*. This shift will greatly enhance our connections with people, who resent being treated as things, and of course they are right because they are more than things, they are relationships and they are sacred. We are not freestanding entities, because on our own, we do not mean or amount to anything — any more than does this book. We only mean something when we are in relationship with each other.

If God made us in His own image, and if God is in everything and every-one and everywhere — then when I look into your face, I am looking into the eyes of God. The face of every parcener, customer, supplier, regulator, and competitor is also the face of God. If we treat each other accordingly, if we serve each other as if we were each God, we would inspire each other with every word and action every day. What's more, much of the packaging and superficiality of modern organizations would be irrelevant. Mission, vision and values statements, customer service and quality programs, diversity, empowerment, and health and safety programs would either be reinvented or eliminated. After all, if I see the face of God when I look into your face, why would I need a *program*? I know what to do. I will serve. This is the way of the mystic, of the servant-leader, of the Inspirational Leader.

All this puts in question our naive pursuit of "the excellent company." In a survey of more than 100,000 employees at twenty-four large companies over twenty-five years, Gallup concluded that units attained the highest levels of organizational performance where employees were the happiest. What old story leaders will find unsettling about this data is that it showed mixed evidence as to the positive effects on performance gained from "corporate culture"; it seems the significant variable for organizational effectiveness is not the corporate culture but the individual leader. In one of the companies surveyed, an international restaurant chain, only 40% of the employees reported being happy, yet some of the highest scores occurred within the same organization, reflecting the positive effect of individual leaders, despite the wider "culture."[7] Organizations don't achieve outcomes, people do. They do it by building relationships — one person at a time.

This turns another set of widely held assumptions about leadership on its head. Programs to achieve, "culture change," "organizational transformation," "interventions" and the like, seldom last, and now we know why. Organizations don't exist, so anything "we do to them" cannot last, either. What lasts are the relationships built between Inspirational Leaders and parceners.

What we are all yearning for is a sense of community, to belong, to experience our kinship with each other. We want to feel safe, to let our guard down, to feel nourished and sacred. Elsewhere I have described these sacred communities of shared values and spirit as Sanctuaries.[8] Teams, departments, divisions, or corporations are simply different-sized Sanctuaries or communities. Communities can range from the very small to the very big: a city block, a hospital, a government — even a country. The rules for community building are the same as the ones we learned in the very first community to which we belonged — the family.

- Do whatever you do as well as you possibly can — Mastery
- In a way that is good for people — Chemistry
- In the service of others — Delivery[9]

The word *community* means a series of relationships. By becoming aware that we are communities, not organizations, we will change the very nature of our relationships, making them less material and more spiritual, less mechanical and more divine, less temporary and more infinite, less cursory and more vital. Then our communities will come alive. Our natural longing to form lasting connections will then transform our affairs — and our planet.

The Paradox of Teams

One of the enduring paradoxes of our time is our commitment to teams and to the rights of the individual at the same time. Like so many others, I have often wrestled with how to pull these seemingly opposing notions together.

As Peter Drucker has pointed out, "No team (except for Gilbert and Sullivan) has ever accomplished anything of importance. The great musicians did not work in teams. The same is true of painters, sculptors, poets, and to a great extent, people who built businesses." Now you may view this as the hyperbole of a lovable and brilliant nonagenarian — and perhaps a rather harsh judgment on the likes of Lennon and McCartney or Lewis and Clarke, but history is on Drucker's side. What we need is what works — and that may or may not be teams. It depends on the purpose of an organization and the context in which this is being achieved. But if we believe that teams are appropriate for given situations, then we will need to adapt the organization to fit the team culture. This includes decision making, reward systems, learning styles, communications, leadership, structure, work styles — all of which are different in teams compared to hierarchies that celebrate the individual.

We live in a culture that glorifies personality and celebrity. It is by these criteria that we now measure our success. The contemporary measures are our levels of fame, wealth, beauty, and power — especially "over" others. We have a multiplicity of incentives for individual performance, even revering it in our constitution and our rights and freedoms. Corporate leaders retell the stories of the great individual competitors — the heroes of our sports, corporate, and entertainment industries — and then extol the virtues of teamwork. While they urge teamwork, payroll thinking remains doggedly resistant to rewarding co-operation, collaboration, and relationships — all essentials of team behavior.

More than anything else, teamwork should be about community, relationships, trust, and love. Ego, the encouragement of individual ambition in search of rewards, is incompatible with group performance and fostering the networks of community, let alone the needs of the soul. Teams compete in win-lose combinations — "my team against yours"; communities flourish with win-win relationships. If we want team-

The greatest strength is gentleness.

IROQUOIS SAYING

work, we will need to structure for it and reward it. In the end, though, we must ask ourselves, "Can I grow on my own? Do I need a relationship with other souls to help me grow?" And we may need to remember that contrary to contemporary fads around this subject, teams may not always be the right answer — we may need to think more in terms of much wider relationships, communities, and Sanctuaries.

The Distance between the Elite and the Street

It is 1979, a basketball game in the Brandeis [University] gym. The team is doing well, and the student section begins a chant, "We're number one! We're number one!" Morrie is sitting nearby. He is puzzled by the cheer.
At one point, in the midst of "We're number one!"
he rises and yells, "What's wrong with being number two?"

The students look at him. They stop chanting. He sits down, smiling and triumphant.
FROM TUESDAYS
WITH MORRIE
BY MITCH ALBOM

There is a growing gulf between the leaders' perception of the work world and that of parceners. One measure of these two solitudes can be found in the statistics of hours worked in America. According to the U.S. Labor Department survey of business establishments, the average workweek shrank from thirty-nine hours in the fifties and early sixties to thirty-five hours in the nineties. Tell that to just about any employee today, and they will think you just got off a spaceship. Their disbelieving impressions are supported by the surveys of Lou Harris & Associates, which show that the median number of hours worked per week has risen from 40.3 per week in 1973 to 50.6 in 1995.[10] Researchers have found that managers simply don't know how hard their employees are working, believing that the old watermark of thirty-five hours still prevails. The truth is, many leaders have no idea how many hours employees invest on their own time or on their computers at home.

Not only are many managers detached from

the realities of employee life, employees are also not thrilled with their leadership experience. A survey in December 1998 by Kepner-Tregoe Inc. of Princeton, New Jersey, asked how employees felt their organization was managed — like a symphony orchestra, a medieval kingdom, or a three-ring circus. A kingdom or a circus was chosen by 59% of supervisors and 72% of employees.

The same study reported 38% of managers and 47% of employees being dissatisfied with their jobs.[11] Such disconnects between leaders and parceners are dangerous — for the relationship between them, for organizational effectiveness, and for families and communities. This was confirmed in another Kepner-Tregoe survey, which reported that 61% of managers and 65% of employees frequently discuss leaving their current employer. Old story leaders are putting at risk the spiritual and emotional well-being of the souls in their organizations if they ignore these danger signals.

In so many aspects of leadership, we focus on *our* perception of reality and what will achieve *our* material ends, seldom considering the *needs of the spirit, or spirits with whom we are partnering* — our parceners, customers, or suppliers. When we ask leaders to define leadership, and then ask their employees the same question — the difference is astonishing. It is the difference between the elite and the street. Leaders will tell you that the hallmarks of great corporate leadership include having a clear vision, defining strategic goals, being decisive, winning in the marketplace, dominating the competition, hiring brilliant people, and motivating them. Ask their parceners the same question and hardly any of the leaders' criteria will be included. Instead, they will tell you they want their leaders to be great mentors and teachers, to be fair and respectful of people and the planet, to act with integrity and to practice high standards of values, to be good listeners, to show compassion, and to communicate well.

We each have egos — those little voices inside that reference our personalities to the outside world, asking, "Am I beautiful?" "Am I loved?" "Will I succeed?" "Can I get more?" Each of us is a unique ego, and often we compete with the egos of others. Our egos are like waves in the sea. We roll along on the surface, doing valuable things until we eventually flare out onto the beach. We don't go away — we return to the ocean — the Universal Soul, which is the sum of every soul of every living thing in the Universe. Eventually a new wave arrives — another ego. But our egos always return to the ocean, the Universal Soul — the oneness of the Divine, like the waves to the ocean. We need to see ourselves in the appropriate perspective — a small but potent wave that is an important part of a much larger picture. We don't disappear or fade away; we simply return to the Whole from which we came in the beginning. We have one body not two, embracing our egos *and* our souls. We cannot separate them. We can only pretend to.

It is an illusion that the goals of personality — increasing shareholder value or "becoming the dominant player in our industry," for example — will lift the hearts of parceners. The goals of personality are like the waves in the ocean; they are important, but not the bigger picture. As Bill George, CEO of Medtronic, points out, "Shareholder value is a hollow notion as the sole source of employee motivation. If you do business that way, you end up like ITT." This comment comes from the Inspirational Leader of a company that makes 50% of the world's pacemakers and many other implantable medical devices. Every employee receives a bronze medallion inscribed with the company's mission, "To alleviate pain, restore health, extend life." The company revels in unabashedly emotional activities like holding a party each year where patients, their families, and doctors are flown in to tell employees how their products saved their lives. Half of corporate revenues come from products introduced in the last twelve months — and the company's total return to shareholders has averaged about 34% over the last decade.[12] It is not that the return to shareholders is unimportant; it is just that it is not the most important thing, and it alone cannot lift the hearts of parceners.

Market Vision, a Canadian market research company, polled consumers to determine the ranking of their personal priorities. Topping the list are job creation, crime prevention, affordable and accessible healthcare, the environment, and programs to protect abused women. At the bottom of the list are support for community and recreational events, amateur sports and — the beer companies will not be pleased to hear this — support for professional sports.[13] An Inspirational Leader seeks to reach people, and does so by addressing the interests that engage the hearts and emotions of others — consumers *and* parceners. Research like this suggests that the leaders of beer companies might communicate more effectively with their markets and therefore inspire their employees if they shifted resources from promoting contact sports to sponsoring bottle and can recycling programs or programs that work with abused women and their abusers.

How did such a great discrepancy occur between the leaders' and parceners' descriptions of great leadership? If parceners are the customers of what leaders are offering, how could the gap between offering and need be so great? If we were to misread the needs of external customers to the same degree, we would have a marketing catastrophe on our hands. Do we have a leadership catastrophe on our hands?

Recently I spoke to a group of managers. My speech was sandwiched between motivational messages and media clips from the corporate president outlining new sales targets, incentive programs, and bonus plans designed to achieve greater levels of output and profit. As the conference closed, I signed books for audience members. After everyone had left, the president turned to me and asked, "Why do people surround you like this, asking questions and having you sign their books?" I said that it happens that way every time. "Why?" she asked. I asked her permission to be frank, and she agreed. "Most of your time was spent talking about *your* needs," I explained. "Most of mine was spent talking about *theirs*. People are yearning to hear that others genuinely care about *their* needs as much as they do. When we show that we care about them, that we understand our role as servant-leaders, then they will exceed our sales targets."

The perfect relationship between the Inspirational Leader and the parcener exists when what the parcener needs is what the Inspirational Leader most wants to give.

Treating Parceners like Customers

The single most critical business issue facing corporate leaders in the medium to long term will be finding the right numbers of qualified employees. In a survey of 1,443 members of TEC (formerly The Executive Committee), an international organization of CEOs, respondents cited hiring, training, and retaining employees as their chief problems. Painful shortages already exist in crucial sectors such as technology and many craft professions. The semiconductor industry alone is forecasting a shortage of forty thousand technical workers in the next five years.[14] Of course, if old story leaders continue to run organizations in ways that alienate people and diminish their souls, the problem of finding good people will simply become more acute — for them at least. It's really very simple: we need to ask people what they want us to do in order to inspire them, and then do it. If we don't, they will simply work somewhere else, following new story leaders wherever they are. We need to understand that all people, whether they are parceners, customers, or suppliers, add value when they are valued.

It will help if we redefine the relationships at work. In a knowledge-based society, power shifts. Managers no longer have all the information. In fact, information rests more with parceners than with managers. In effect, this changes their status into volunteers — they work in your organization, not because they need to, but because they want to — they volunteer to. The Inspirational Leader takes great care to find out what draws volunteers to particular work environments and then replicates this as faithfully as possible.

During the last forty years, we have become experts at identifying the needs of customers. In the process, we have spawned entire fields of inquiry and practice such as marketing, selling, customer service, and quality. We have learned to perfect the science of identifying needs and motivating customer response. What potential could we unleash with parceners before launching initiatives that affect them, if we used these same sophisticated marketing techniques — double-blind studies, focus groups, market testing, empirical research, and the like? What would be the happy result of investing the same level of sophistication, innovation, financial capital, and sensitivity in our parceners as we routinely do with customers? The art of leadership might become as effective as the art of marketing. We need to consider doing something too few leaders do today — to look at leadership through the eyes of the parcener-as-customer. When we realize that parceners are customers, too, and accurately identify and meet their needs, they will rise to unparalleled performance. A new science is about to be born.

SAS Institute Inc., the highly successful software company founded by Jim Goodnight, indulges its parceners with a 36,000-square-foot gym, including an expansive hardwood aerobics floor, two full-sized basketball courts, exercise and workout areas, and a skylit yoga room. The company maintains soccer and softball fields, offers massages and classes in golf, African dance, tennis, and tai chi and will launder workout clothes and return them the next day. Today, SAS has more than 5,400 employees on its Cary, North Carolina, campus — up from 1,900 employees five years ago and ten times as many since the company was formed fifteen years ago. In its early days, some of SAS's most highly trained female staff members left the company because they were unable to find adequate daycare. The company reacted by providing daycare in the basement for five children. Today, there are 528 children in the facility, which is the largest on-site daycare in North Carolina.[15] As I stood beside the lake on the campus grounds, I was struck by the serenity of the place — inside and out — unusual in the frenzied world of technology. Azalea and rhododendron bushes cascade down to the boardwalk that surrounds the lake. Employees are encouraged to swim, boat and picnic, and not to work past 5 p.m.! The clusters of low-rise buildings are nestled in the rolling campus hills, among tall ponderosa pines and shade trees. I paused to watch a snapping turtle sun itself on a bridge footing. "I've never seen anything like this in my career," says Martin Bourque, a ten-year SAS veteran.

One of the benefits of this largesse is low staff turnover. Whereas staff turnover in technology companies can typically average 20% a year (equal to about 1,000 employees for SAS), only 130 leave SAS, resulting in almost 900 employees that they do not need to replace. Employee turnover averages about 3.7% currently and has never exceeded 5%. The company offers no stock option, and salaries are generally slightly below or equal to industry norms. Yet employees are dedicated, loyal, and committed to the organization. Another benefit of treating parceners like customers is performance — all but two of the hundred largest U.S. corporations are customers of SAS.

When Quint Studer became president of Baptist Hospital in Pensacola, Florida, the facility ranked in the bottom nineteenth percentile in customer satisfaction as measured by Press, Gainey of South Bend, Indiana. Two years later, hospitals in the Baptist Health Care system ranked numbers one, two, and three in patient satisfaction out of six hundred hospitals surveyed nationwide. They now run weekly benchmarking days for a stream of hospital executives eager to learn how they achieved this stunning turnaround. Says Studer, "People around here thought I had been hired to improve patient satisfaction, but I didn't even mention patient satisfaction for the first few months." Instead, he focused directly on asking parceners what their needs were and meeting them — everything from full disclosure of financial and management information, more authority for ordering supplies, faster emergency-room psychiatric assessments, night cafeteria service, coordinating security and nursing shifts (so nurses could be escorted to their cars at night), quarterly employee discussion forums and leadership development coaching. Charts kept on parcener and customer satisfaction data tell the story — as soon as parcener satisfaction improved, customer satisfaction did, too — the rise in the curves is almost identical. The patient service improvement program is working, but it is working because the parcener service improvement program is working. This is how Baptist Health System became the best practice hospital for patient satisfaction in America.

O, how full of briars is the working-day world!

ROSALIND

IN AS YOU LIKE IT BY WILLIAM SHAKESPEARE

The Old Story: Testosterone Leadership

The only
solution is
to love.

DOROTHY DAY

It didn't look like a business conference. An entire Asian-region management team was dressed in black army fatigues, combat boots and berets, and "guarded" by staff dressed in fatigues and black balaclava helmets. The *Mission Impossible* theme blared from speakers, underscoring the challenge of repeating the previous year's growth of 70%. I scanned the program. The lunch invitation read, "1200: Eat lunch or be eaten."

I found my host and alerted him that I feared my message would conflict with his, perhaps undermining the company's strategy or throwing off their meeting agenda. He told me not to worry. I walked to the podium, and gamely started my speech by making references to "peaceful warriors," a popular term, but one that I view as phony because it is an oxymoron. Was Buddha a peaceful warrior?

As I progressed, I knew that I could not present a discussion on the importance of truth-telling without being honest myself. I improvised a little, explaining that I was the yin to balance the yang of their agenda. I asked the audience if they believed we should kill people at work and if their repeated chants about dominating the market were really serving their customers' needs, or just those of their egos. I gently suggested to them that even if dominating the market was important to them, it was probably irrelevant to customers.

So here I was, on the other side of the globe, faced with an eerie paradox: I was in Singapore, a Westerner working in the East with Easterners, who were promoting the worst aspects of Western culture — aggression and violence — and I was now urging them to restore and embrace their natural Eastern values. A dropped pin would have been thunderous.

My speech finished, I prepared to be railroaded out of Singapore. First a few people, then the majority of the audience, told me how uncomfortable they were with the war metaphor and militaristic bombast, how they had grudgingly agreed with it, but how closely my message mirrored their true beliefs. They welcomed a message that drew from and aligned so closely with their cultural wisdom: the teachings of Buddha, Confucius, and the Tao. They were not critical of management, believing them to be on autopilot and using the tired metaphors of violence and war universally employed by old story leaders of global organizations.

Here's a secret. Inspiration to greatness comes from love, not war. A call to arms is not an effective way to engage the hearts and souls of parceners. Try to picture the leader of the Boston Symphony getting up in the morning and ranting, "Let's destroy the Los Angeles Symphony." This is "testosterone leadership." No one needs to die, and we don't need to take prisoners or scorch the earth. There is room for us all. Innovation, creativity, synergy, collaboration, teamwork and, above all else, love, will lead to mastery and therefore our success.

To fear love is to fear life.

BERTRAND RUSSELL

We may not always notice the subtle changes that are being signaled to us. For example, the old story is that there are almost as many guns in North America as there are people. The new story is that fewer people own one. A New York City jury recently found fifteen handgun manufacturers liable in the shootings of seven people there. These trends signal the arrival of the new story — indicating the critical mass that is forming. Violence is a bankrupt model of inspiration. The old story drew on the examples of war, domination, violence, victory, and rugged individualism.

The sword conquered for a while, but the spirit conquers for ever!

SHOLEM ASCH

People yearn for leaders who will serve them, not kill them — who are not Lone Rangers but who build communities. Ten thousand years from now we will remember the name of Nelson Mandela, not Lee Iacocca.

Love alone is capable of uniting living beings in such a way as to complete and fulfill them, for it alone takes them and joins them by what is deepest in themselves.

PIERRE TEILHARD DE CHARDIN

Leadership training is entering a new phase. The new story of leadership is based on nurturing, teaching, growing, caring, listening, empathizing, and respecting. Mentors and leaders are those who love their parceners. The new story will look to the wisdom of Christian, Native American, and Eastern values and beliefs, and is based on life-affirming — not life-threatening — models. Just ask your parceners — they are the customers of leaders.

The Millennium Effect

Science rules our Western thinking. We are entranced by technology, but we have lost our sense of romance, instinct, and intuition. We are entering a time of balance between the mind and the heart, between the personality and the soul. However, many modern organizations are still ruled by the mind, and their leaders are intent on changing the behavior of others through the use of science — double-blind studies, market research, opinion polls and surveys, all in the name of corroborating their philosophies with "hard, empirical data." "If it can't be measured, it does not exist," goes the mantra of the strategy theorists. Some consider the romantic view of work and life as sentimental and "non-business-like." But the romantic view of work and life is inspiring — often much more so than pragmatic, scientific analysis. Inspirational Leaders know that there is room for both. We can invite our souls to soar on the wings of an idea powered by passion and intuition just as easily as we can implement "a program." We can make room in our hearts and minds for noble ideas that include science but also transcend it. Thoughts fueled by passion and inspiration are charged with as much, often more, spiritual energy than those driven solely by the sciences and technologies of our time. To the Inspirational Leader, romance is as important, perhaps even more so, than process. Did Christ, Buddha, Gandhi, Martin Luther King, or Confucius know about the technologies of interpersonal skills?

Quite often we become so enraptured with our science, that it seems to assume a life and purpose of its own. A contemporary example is our millennium romance. The year 2000 evokes a global emotion, engaging people in an almost mythical way. Yet, a millennium is a figment of our imagination, an artificial artifact spun from the human mind.

> **We are shaped and fashioned by what we love.**
>
> JOHANN WOLF-GANG VON GOETHE

> **Science has made the world a neighborhood, but it will take love to make it a sisterhood, a brotherhood, a community of peace and justice.**
>
> ELIZABETH M. SCOTT

The Millennial Romance

Time is a human idea. The Gregorian Calendar in use today is just one of many systems for measuring time around the world. Though widely used now, it is a relative newcomer to human consciousness, having only been in general use since 1582. Almost six thousand years ago, the Egyptians pioneered the use of the solar year and in 45 BC, Sosigenes, an astronomer from Alexandria, persuaded Julius Caesar to use the sun as an arbiter of time. Things stayed much this way for centuries, in large part because the Roman Catholic Church branded scholars like Roger Bacon, a thirteenth-century English philosopher and scientist, as heretics, even though he had calculated that the Julian Calendar was out of sync with the solar rhythms by one day every 125 years. In the sixth century, a monk named Dionysius Exiguus (Dennis the Short) established the basis for today's calendar. Historians now believe, however, that Christ was born no later than 4 BC, the year that King Herod died.

Meanwhile, Native North Americans were oblivious to all this scientific and religious controversy because in their consciousness there was no concept of linear time — for them time was circular. The seasons revolved, returning to be enjoyed again and again — like a sort of carousel. In the year AD 2000, the Jewish calendar reads 5760, the Islamic calendar 1420 and the Chinese calendar 4698 — to name but three examples.

So why has the year 2000 taken on such significance for us? It can only be the result of our human need to infuse ritual with high levels of passion and mysticism. We could have measured time by the moon or by eclipses or tides, or perhaps not even measured time at all. We have created a paradox: it is clear that the very idea of a millennium is intellectually or scientifically absurd; that it is emotionally and spiritually real is also just as true.

The psychic power of the millennium is easy to understand. Many people make New Year's resolutions; many more make them, in fact, than keep them. Psychologically, the responsibility attached to making similar commitments at the end of a century is palpably greater. The power of suggestion and sheer awe attached to making a resolution at the end of the millennium thus becomes almost mythical. This is an opportunity never to be repeated, not just in our lifetimes, but in those of some sixty future generations. Putting it this way causes us to approach the responsibility being placed on us with great awe and humility; we should ensure our resolutions are the right ones and that we abide by them. It is a time for us to question many of society's touchstones, to cast out sacred cows and to embrace different values that will better serve our dreams for the future.

Above all, it is a time of optimism because we have been presented with a once-in-a-lifetime gift, the chance to replace rapacity with reverence in our relations with each other and the planet. We are being called upon to get it right, and because we will not get another chance, we must make resolutions that are of an order of magnitude greater than any lower-level ones, such as previous New Year's, or even *fin-de-siècle* resolutions. The millennium acts as a universal mirror that is being held up to each of us, and some of us are scared by what we see, and it is not a temporary thing — the beginning of a millennium is measured in decades.

The Omega Point Meets the Critical Mass

The millennium offers us an unusual leadership opportunity. It may be completely illogical, but we should nevertheless accept this priceless gift. The millennium energy has created an awareness and opened the hearts and kindled the hopes of millions of people who genuinely believe that the time may be right for a radical redesign of leadership, organizations and work. Ten years ago, such ambitious aspirations would not have been possible.

Pierre Teilhard de Chardin, a Jesuit priest and eminent paleontologist, wrote about what he called the *noosphere*. In *The Phenomenon of Man*, he wrote, "Evolution is a general condition to which all theories, all hypotheses, all systems must bow and which they must satisfy henceforward if they are to be thinkable and true. Evolution is a light illuminating all facts." He argued that matter has always obeyed "that great law of biology... the law of 'complexification.' "[16] He postulated that the matter-energy of the Universe, since the beginning of time, has continued to evolve into greater complexity. Humanity, he believed, introduced a new level of complexity, while at the same time moving evolution to a new dimension. Teilhard described a many-layered biosphere covering the Earth (the Earth's internal cores, the outer crust and soil, the oceans, lakes and rivers, the flora and fauna, the atmosphere) from which emerged the noosphere (an envelope of intellect surrounding the earth). This mind layer, or human consciousness, leads to a higher consciousness, and as this evolutionary process unfolds, the material and the spiritual converge into a superconsciousness. Teilhard called this moment when life becomes self-aware, *The Omega Point* — the moment in time when information is universally present within the human consciousness. It is through love that this God-Omega directs the continuation of the whole evolutionary process.

Another way of understanding this is to consider the term *critical mass*, a scientific term (meaning the smallest mass of material that will maintain a permanent change) that gained wider currency when James Redfield wrote about it in *The Celestine Prophecy*.

Love is the poetry of the senses.

HONORÉ DE BALZAC

Critical mass occurs when awareness of a new body of knowledge becomes so widespread that it displaces the existing body of knowledge. James Redfield's name for the Omega Point was the *First Insight*, the creation of a critical mass when large numbers of people realize that they are experiencing a convergence of information and shared opinions.

The Hundredth Monkey

Lyall Watson and Ken Kesey, who wrote separately about the Hundredth Monkey Phenomenon, described an example of critical mass at work.[17] According to Watson, scientists had been observing the Japanese monkey, *Macaca fuscata*, as part of a lengthy research project for over thirty years. In 1952, on the island of Koshima, scientists were providing monkeys with sweet potatoes placed in the sand. The monkeys enjoyed the taste of the raw sweet potatoes but disliked the accompanying dirt. An eighteen-month-old female, Imo, solved the problem by washing the potatoes in a nearby stream. She taught this trick to her mother. Her playmates also learned this new way and they taught their mothers, too.

The scientists observed more and more of the monkeys adopting this cultural innovation. Between 1952 and 1958, all the young monkeys had learned to wash the sandy sweet potatoes to make them more palatable. Only the adults who imitated their children learned this social improvement. Other adults kept eating the dirty sweet potatoes.

Then something startling took place in 1958. One autumn morning, about ninety-nine of the monkeys from Koshima were washing their sweet potatoes. Later that morning, the one-hundredth monkey learned to wash potatoes. At this point, a sort of spontaneous intellectual combustion occurred. By evening, almost every monkey in the tribe was washing sweet potatoes before eating them. The added energy of this one-hundredth monkey somehow created a breakthrough in consciousness! But that's not all. The most surprising thing observed by the scientists was that the habit of washing sweet potatoes then spontaneously jumped over the sea —

colonies of monkeys on other islands and the mainland troop of monkeys at Takasakiyama began washing their sweet potatoes, too!

The Hundredth Monkey Phenomenon is a myth, but it is retold as if it were genuine, over and over again. As Lyall Watson wrote in *Whole Earth Review*, "It is a metaphor of my own making, based... on very slim evidence and a great deal of hearsay." Even though the Hundredth Monkey Phenomenon is a myth, the message it contains is so compelling, people all over the world *want* it to be true, because in our hearts we know it to be so.

How Critical Mass Is Shaping Marketing

All over the world, a convergence of concern and a desire for new thinking — you can call it a critical mass, an Omega Point, a Hundredth Monkey Phenomenon, or an "abundance outlook" — is growing in human awareness. These are not just the concerned views of fringe thinkers anymore. There now exists, as never before, a powerful universal desire to set our former follies behind us and to behave responsibly to each other and to the planet, before it is too late. The millennium is a symbol of this critical mass — it is an intellectual gathering place.

We now agree what the problems are: there is insufficient soul integrity among our leaders; too many old story leaders are still peddling old story potions and snake-oil: we are failing to inspire parceners, and people are yearning for Inspirational Leaders to show the way forward. A growing spiritual hunger burns in the breasts of parceners. Our ideas for solutions are now clear. The last piece of the jigsaw puzzle is the agreement on how we act, how we lead, and how we inspire in these times — in short, how we become Inspirational Leaders.

One of the many indicators of the shifts in thinking being brought about by this growing critical mass, is the way some forward-thinking leaders view marketing today. Business schools have for years taught models that include strategies for pricing and distribution that enable the market maker to dominate the market — an old story philosophy of scarcity. Inevitably, high prices and limited alternatives result, until similar products become available, thus transferring more power to consumers. Now think of Netscape. This company was founded on the concept of giving their principal product away — a philosophy of abundance. The underlying theory was that if potential customers bought the product, many software developers would write programs for it, thus making it the industry standard. The strategy worked — Netscape's Internet browser became the preferred offering, out-selling Microsoft's comparable product, the Internet Explorer, and industry standards were set.

Another example is the remarkable story of Linus Torvalds. When Torvalds was ten years old, his grandfather brought home a Commodore VIC-20, on which the boy began writing computer games. In 1991, while studying at the University of Helsinki, he invented an operating system for his personal computer that he preferred to the operating system he was using (Microsoft's DOS) and to the one used by the university (Unix). He called it Linux (rhymes with cynics). Instead of becoming an impossibly rich techno-guru, he did something different — he gave the software away on the Internet, including the source code that programmers use to create software. Today, the number of machines running on Linux exceeds ten million, certainly a long way behind Microsoft Window's 374 million users, but growing at greater than 20% a year, thanks to millions of dedicated volunteer programmers who contribute daily improvements and add-ons to the software. Most of these programmers have never met, communicating internationally by e-mail. Linux is a sort of meritocracy — code-written, for it is scrutinized closely by peers, and only the most rigorous is adopted and incorporated into the master program. Torvalds, who is just twenty-eight, has moved his family from Finland to Silicone Valley to join Transmeta Corp., a top-secret technology start-up partly funded by Microsoft co-founder, Paul Allen. Linux has gone mainstream — it was used to run special effects for the movie *Titanic*. Oracle is offering Linux versions of some of its database management software. Sun Microsystems uses the program for low-end workstations, and Datapro, a technology research firm, reports that Linux receives the highest rating for professional operating systems from users.[18] New story leader Torvalds views competition and scarcity as irrelevant. New story thinking views life in terms of communities and abundance — and the result is more for everyone.

Sociologist Paul Ray recently surveyed Americans and discovered that 24% of them (forty-four million) are idealistic and spiritual; are concerned about relationships and psychological development; are concerned about the environment; and are open to creating a positive future.[19] He called this group "cultural creatives." A critical mass within a population is generally considered to be 1% or higher — the number of people who are interested in non-material reality far surpasses this. The new story is well underway.

When we turn on electric lights, nothing seems to happen for the first seven-eighths of the switch's movement. It is only during the last eighth of the movement that the light turns on. During the first seven-eighths of the movement, we could mistakenly conclude that nothing was happening. But our impatience would be a misunderstanding — lights turn on as a result of the entire eight-eighths of the movement of the switch. In terms of our awareness about leadership, we are now in the last eighth of the process of learning and development. To some, it may appear that little is happening, but the lights are about to turn on. When they do, it will be called Enlightenment.

The Three Ages of Power

Power has been at the core of the human experience since the beginning of time. It has shaped our understanding of the leadership archetype (an ideal example of a type from the Greek *archi* + *tupos* "model, stamp"). Organizations and their leaders have accumulated power; individuals have struggled against it and for it. The result is an alienating powerlessness that has led individuals and societies from disappointment and unhappiness to anarchy and violence. Power has become a currency of exchange between egos.

Old story thinking argues that the will to hold power is a human urge that, at best, can be subjugated but never eradicated. There have been many proponents of this view, among them Sigmund Freud, Friedrich Nietzsche, Jean-Paul Sartre, and Alfred Adler. They argue that enough is never enough to satisfy humans. Furthermore, power has a life of its own and seeks its own survival. This argument ignores the notion that power is the result, not the cause, of human behavior.

Until now, this view has been the working paradigm for many fields of human relationships, including leadership. However, the nature of power has changed over time, and yet another major evolution in the nature of power is occurring today. Over the last four thousand years, we have passed through two distinct patterns of power, and now a third pattern is emerging. I divide these phases of power into three ages:

1. The Age of Arian Power
2. The Age of Piscean Power
3. The Age of Aquarian Power

There are no schools for leaders. Leadership is something we learn informally on the job as we mimic others in a learning-by-doing school of apprenticeship. Often, leadership is thrust upon us and, as a consequence, each of us defines our own leadership archetype.

The Age of Arian Power

Astrologers refer to the two thousand years before the birth of Christ as the Age of Aries. Aries is the first sign of the zodiac and is symbolized by the ram. According to astrologers, Aries, a fire sign, is ruled by the planet Mars, named for the Roman god of war. The Greeks adopted Aries as a war god, although they had no real love of war. Many Greek deities, especially Athena, the goddess of wisdom, despised Aries.

Mars, the Roman equivalent of Aries, personified violence and battle. Roman image-makers portrayed Mars as an armed warrior, replete with spear and shield, and he was frequently associated with Bellona, the Roman goddess of war. Chariot races, which often ended in bloody rituals, barbarous executions, and the sacrifice of animals, were some of the primary events at festivals held in his honor in March (named for him) and October. To the Romans, Mars was one of the most important deities, revered as the father of the Roman people, because he was the father of Romulus, the legendary founder of Rome. To commemorate his victory over the assassins of Julius Caesar in 42 BC, Emperor Augustus honored Mars with the cult title *Ultor* (Avenger) and a new temple.

The warrior and avenger archetype represented leadership style throughout the two thousand years prior to the birth of Christ. This was an age of extreme daily violence in which brutality, physical outrage, and force were the principal means by which those with power achieved their ends — the domination of others. The goal of most people in these times was to survive in this hostile world filled with human predators, where power was the principal commodity of human existence.

The Warrior: The Arian Leader Archetype

The Arian leader is *The Warrior*. This is a leader who says, "I am your leader. Follow me, I know the way!" History has produced many Arian leaders, among them Oliver Cromwell, Charlemagne, Alexander the Great, Napoleon Bonaparte, Attila the Hun, Genghis Khan, Karl Marx, Mao Tse-Tung, Leon Trotsky, and Vladimir Ilyich Lenin. All prosecuted power through violence.

Today, the entertainment and media industries are the main creators and custodians of much of our contemporary leadership iconography. The

O.J. Simpson trial in 1990 added more than $200 million to the GDP of America (more than, say, the GDP of Grenada). We are captivated by film and television machismo, as portrayed by Clint Eastwood, John Wayne, Mel Gibson, or Sean Penn. These "warriors" are almost exclusively male, white, decisive, and materially successful. Above all they are heroic. In the music sector of the entertainment industry, the models are Marilyn Manson, Buddy Holly, Jimi Hendrix, Kurt Cobain, Johnny Cash, and Alice Cooper — not always white this time, but still male, heroic, warriors. Spectator sports, a branch of the entertainment industry, offers yet more images of the same: Dennis Rodman, John McEnroe, Mike Tyson, and Don Cherry. They embody the values of rugged individualism, frontier courage and stamina, pioneer spirit, and the drive to succeed and win.

Today, corporate executives frequently cast themselves in the image of the warrior-leader, rallying their parceners with battle cries about crushing the competition and conquering markets in a world they see as filled with pillagers, opponents, dangers, and antagonists. We speak, use the phrases and fashions, and study the psychology of these warrior-hero icons. "Show me the money" is heard more often on Wall Street than the Jerry McGuire character (played by Tom Cruise) could ever have imagined.

> **Every Communist must grasp the truth, "Political power grows out of the barrel of a gun."**
> MAO TSE-TUNG

It is no coincidence that 40% of all homicides portrayed on network television are perpetrated by corporate executives. It would be difficult to take programs seriously if 40% of teachers, nurses, doctors, pilots, or law enforcement officers were murderers, but the public will readily accept that this proportion of homicides could be committed by corporate executives. Some 30% of top corporate executives, according to research by a world-class psychiatric teaching hospital, are potentially psychopaths. We have taken as our leadership archetypes — our role models — a bizarre representation that is beginning to frighten and alienate parceners, and the public at large.

> **Communism is Soviet power plus the electrification of the whole country.**
> VLADIMIR ILYICH LENIN

At its best, the warrior-leader archetype is admired as an example of the rugged spirit that built a nation, and at its worst, as an anachronism in an age that yearns for a more mature and sensitive leadership style.

The problem with the warrior-leader archetype is that it is built on a foundation of envy. It benefits the heroic warrior-leader most, not the parcener. Of course, powerful, jet-setting, wealthy executives like the late

Steve Ross of Time-Warner, Tony O'Reilly, the former CEO of Heinz, or Disney's Michael Eisner, may make $40 million in annual compensation, but the real question is whether the same levels of intellectual, spiritual, and material nourishment are being enjoyed by their parceners. If leadership is about unlocking the potential of humans, which humans are we talking about? Is the heroism of the warrior-leader the best, or even a relevant benchmark with which to measure leadership effectiveness?

Our confusion between effectiveness, fantasy, and subjectivity yields surprising results. When Lee Iacocca was chairman of Chrysler Corp., he was frequently touted as an ideal candidate for president of the United States. Shortly after his retirement, *Fortune* magazine wrote an article about his loneliness and depression: the warrior-leader archetype model is weak. Al "Chainsaw" Dunlap of Scott Paper and Sunbeam corporations, the poster boy of the warrior-leader archetype, became famous for his sound bites such as, "If you want a friend, get a dog" and "You're in business for one thing, to make money. If you have another agenda, join Rotary." Celebrated by some as a cost-cutting, turn-around expert and brilliant leader, but vilified by others as a heartless, slash-and-burn executive with no other skills in his toolbox, he was eventually fired by angry shareholders. The president of Coca-Cola asked a *Fortune* magazine reporter the rhetorical question, "What do you do when your competitor is drowning?" His answer: "Get a live hose and stick it in his mouth."

Many leaders assume "attitude" as part of their persona, and they are proud of this. But parceners are yearning for leaders *without* attitude. Persona comes from a word that means *mask* — and parceners are tired of dealing with masks. They want real people in their lives; people who are vulnerable, emotional, spiritual, and lovable. They yearn for leaders who are living in spiritual truth. The enlightened leader, the Inspirational Leader, is a person who has evolved to transcend the separate concepts of the ego and the soul — they understand and live them as one. For the Inspirational Leader, there is no duality, the finite is the infinite — what you see is what you get. The ego becomes congruent with the soul in every aspect of behavior, action, and belief — in every aspect of life, at home, at play, at work.

The Age of Piscean Power

Pisces is the twelfth sign of the zodiac and is symbolized by two fish swimming in opposite directions, a sign shared by Christianity. It is ruled by the planet Neptune, a water sign. The Romans honored Neptune, who was known by the Greeks as Poseidon, the god of the sea. Neptune was the son of the god Saturn, who was a brother of Jupiter, the king of the gods, and of Pluto, the god of the dead and ruler of the underworld.

The Greek god Poseidon personified intellect and power, combined with treachery and deceit. This is best exemplified in Greek mythology by the story of the Trojan War. Eris, goddess of discord, tossed a golden apple among the heavenly guests at the wedding of Peleus. It was inscribed "for the fairest" and was awarded to Aphrodite, the goddess of love, by Paris, son of King Priam of Troy. On this occasion, the beautiful Helen, wife of Menelaus, the king of Sparta, fell in love with Paris and accompanied him to Troy. To avenge this insult, Menelaus assembled a vast force to attack Troy under the command of Agamemnon, king of Mycenae. When the Trojans refused to return Helen to Menelaus, the Greek warriors sailed to Troy in one thousand ships, laying siege to Troy for ten years.

It was Poseidon and Apollo, the god of the sun, who had built the walls of Troy to withstand such attacks. Frustrated by their decade of failure, the Greeks developed an elaborate stratagem. After building a huge, hollow, wooden horse, they left it on the shore near Troy and sailed away. Sinon, a Greek spy, persuaded the Trojans to accept the horse as a gift from the Greeks, arguing that it would make Troy invulnerable. The Trojans fell for this ploy and that night, Sinon let out the armed Greek warriors who were hiding inside the horse. After killing the guards, they opened the gates to the Greeks, who sacked and burned Troy.

The Age of Pisces, the two thousand years since the birth of Christ, was a time in which people were moved by beliefs. This often resulted in institutionalized ideologies, most notably the great religions of the world. Like Arian power, Piscean power seeks to control, but it does so in more subtle ways. Whereas Arian power is exerted through the use of brute force, Piscean power uses instruments of the intellect to dominate others — religion, politics, hierarchies, institutions, legislation, the law, caste and class structures, old-boy networks, racism, genocide, dogma, economics, and trade. Piscean power epitomizes intellectual tribalism, which seeks to exclude those who do not belong. The inevitable clashes of ideology result in oppression and violence. This has been a familiar pattern during the last two thousand years.

The transition from Arian to Piscean power brought a shift from the brutal to the subtle. This shift was noticeable, for instance, with the realization that the subtlety of the pen was mightier than the brutality of the sword. Two notable examples: Charles Dickens' *Tale of Two Cities* and Emile Zola's *J'accuse*, both of which aroused moral outrage against social injustice. Today, many leaders use the Piscean model of power as their own, choosing to lead others through ideological authoritarianism — competition, corporate strategy, mergers and acquisitions, market domination, mindshare, intelligence gathering, and theft being a few of today's corporate examples. For many workers in this environment, the terrain looks dangerous.

The Mentor: The Piscean Leader Archetype

The Piscean leader is *The Mentor*. This is a leader who says, "I am your leader. How can I teach you?" In Greek mythology, Mentor was the elderly friend of Odysseus and tutor of his son Telemachus. Today, the tutor's name has become an eponym for a wise, trustworthy counselor or teacher.

Man's mind, once stretched by a new idea, never regains its original dimensions.

OLIVER WENDELL HOLMES, JR.

Mentors seek to influence the thinking of others. The power of knowledge is the currency of the mentor-leader archetype, who seeks to serve others by guiding their thinking. Mentor-leader archetypes shape the beliefs and attitudes of others and therefore influence and often determine their behavior. They use their power in two ways: first, to suppress information they do not wish parceners to learn, or to hold back knowledge that contradicts their ideologies or teachings; second, to impart knowledge by communicating ideas, concepts, and information to others. The impact of a mentor-leader archetype is permanent because no one remains untouched by information that is new to them. By definition, learning is altered behavior, because we are always altered, even if only a little, as a result of learning. In the extreme, mentor-leader archetypes can be overzealous, seeking to indoctrinate, brainwash, and control information. They sometimes institutionalize their teachings, through religious doctrine and sects, political parties and regimes, ideologies and educational systems, even through advertising, marketing, and fashion trends. In their more wholesome form, mentor-leader archetypes are truly our friends as well as our leaders. They seek to teach, to share, to give, and above all, *to love*. Many mothers, fathers, and siblings are important mentor-leader archetypes. Great educators, artists, and writers are mentor-leader archetypes too. Some of the

If a man empties his purse into his head, no one can take it away from him. An investment in knowledge always pays the best interest.

BENJAMIN FRANKLIN

greatest leaders in history have been mentor-leader archetypes — Abraham, Socrates, Sophocles, Mohammad, Voltaire, Thomas Aquinas, Nicolaus Copernicus, Albert Einstein, Martin Luther, John Wesley, Florence Nightingale, and Susan B. Anthony. The common theme among these mentor-leaders is that they were conscious of their considerable power to influence others. They saw others as a means of extending their own ideas and therefore their power.

The Age of Aquarian Power

Aquarius is the eleventh sign of the zodiac. Characterized as a water bearer, Aquarius is an air sign, ruled by the planet Uranus, whom the Greeks honored as god of the heavens. The wife of Uranus was Gaia, the goddess of Earth. Uranus was the father of the Titans, the Cyclopes, and the 100-handed giants. To the Greeks, the Titans represented earthquakes, volcanic eruptions, and the wildest forces of Nature.

The leader of the Titans was Cronus, the son of Uranus, who dethroned and castrated his father with a sickle,

Where love rules, there is no will to power, and where power predominates, love is lacking. The one is the shadow of the other.

CARL JUNG

thus stealing his power. From the blood that fell upon the earth sprang the Three Furies, the snaky-haired and hideous goddesses of revenge, who lived in the underworld, from which they emerged to pursue and drive mad those committing such heinous crimes as patricide and perjury.

But the initial brutishness of these deities was merely the source of their later enlightenment. When the severed genitals of Uranus fell into the sea, there arose from them and the turbulent foam (*aphros* in Greek) Aphrodite, the goddess of love and beauty, known by the Romans as Venus. The Olympian deities who stood for peace and order eventually overcame the furious and belligerent Titans. The Three Furies gave up vengeful insistence on the ancient law of blood-for-blood and became known as the Kindly Ones.

It is the same in our times. The excesses of violence and aggression displayed by Arian and Piscean leaders are still very evident, but they are waning. Competitive warrior-leader archetype CEOs increasingly appear anachronistic to their parceners. They reason, "If you can kill the competition, will I be the next on your hit list?" This is not a thought to inspire the soul. In the Greek tragedy of Uranus and Cronos, barbarism gave birth to Aphrodite, the goddess of love and beauty. The Titans, like modern humans, relinquished their heritage of chaos and violence in favor of peace and order. The Three Furies became the Kindly Ones. The Age of Aquarius, the age of love and beauty, is descended from the previous ages of competition, fear, and violent power.

Aquarius is a visionary astrological sign. Although the Age of Aquarius dawned in the 1940s, we were not ready for the enlightenment that it presaged. It takes more than fifty years for a new astrological age to take root, and the turn of the new millennium signals the arrival of that time. The idealism of the 1960s was quickly met with a predictable and firm resistance to change from the prevailing paradigm, the intellectual power of the Piscean Age. When Piscean powerbrokers heard the words of James Rado, the New York hippie who in 1967 co-authored the hopeful lyrics from the musical "Hair," they were simply not ready.

You only have power over people as long as you don't take everything away from them. But when you've robbed a man of everything he's no longer in your power — he's free again.

ALEXANDER SOLZHENITSYN

Over the next several hundred years, we will see spiritual transformations unfold that today can only be imagined. Arian and Piscean power sought to exert power over others; Aquarian power is almost exactly the reverse — it seeks to emancipate and invigorate the spiritual power of others. Arian and Piscean power sought to dominate; Aquarian power seeks to liberate. Arian and Piscean power is finite; Aquarian power is infinite. Arian and Piscean power is scarce; Aquarian power is abundant.

The Servant: The Aquarian Leader Archetype

The Aquarian leader is *The Servant*. This is a leader who says, "I am your leader. How can I serve you?"

Many executives focus most of their energy on containment. By containment, I mean building permanent protection from the usual hazards and dangers inherent in all organizations. These executives think of a workforce as something to be reduced, not inspired. Consequently, they focus on monitoring costs, lowering overheads, reducing risks, protecting assets, and making decisions only after gaining the protection of a contract and the advice of legal counsel. This is not leadership, but management, and it is rooted in attitudes based on fear and scarcity instead of love and abundance. Elsewhere, I have defined management as doing things right, and leadership as doing the right thing.[20]

The Aquarian leader is just as aware of power as the Arian or Piscean leader, but where the latter two seek to use their power to dominate others and to steal their power, the Aquarian leader seeks to *give* power to others, to *em*power them. The resulting power is far greater because it is multiplied and fueled by passion. Contrary to our current thinking, the leader loses nothing by giving power away. Indeed, it is, like knowledge, a gift one may bestow without any loss. This is because the Aquarian leader really gives nothing away, but simply enables parceners to become aware of the power they already possess.

In this new story thinking we are not pushed towards greater and greater personal achievements. Instead, we are encouraged to ask others, "How can I be of service to you?" The results are astounding, reshaping the culture of families, organizations, communities, and countries.

The Aquarian Age has placed us in a unique place as we move towards the critical mass. We are experiencing a complete mind-shift, and it is not just leaders that are experiencing it — the phenomenon is universal. There is an awakening among a wide range of people who have come to the realization that fear and power is not only an ineffective way of relating with people, but it is uncivilized, too. In the communities and relationships we call corporations or organizations, fear is also an ineffective way to elicit high performance from others — and it is just as uncivilized there, too. This is not just a neo-awakening, or a reawakening. We are at a historic moment in which our attitude to others is shifting from one based on personality and ego, to one based on the sacredness of our relationships. More and more, we are yearning for spiritual experiences and we are becoming increasingly aware that these can only be achieved through companionship (from the Latin words *com* and *pan*, "with" and "bread" — to share bread together). Spiritual experiences are achieved in the company of other souls.

Inspirational Leader Bonnie Wesorick, founder of CPM Resource Center in Grand Rapids, Michigan, puts it this way, "We had become so task-dominated and saw work as the things we did, not who we were. It's not that we liked it, we didn't know how to break the cycle of barriers to us coming together as human beings (as spiritual beings). ...My work is to create cultures where we honor the human spiritual being."

A teacher affects eternity; he can never tell where his influence stops.

HENRY ADAMS

We are now entering a new era in which power will continue to be as important as ever, but the way we use it will change. We will no longer be preoccupied with the use of power to control and dominate others in order to meet our own ends. Instead, we will awaken to power as something we give to others when we serve them — this is spiritual power. Never before has there been a greater yearning for leaders to serve their parceners.

All leaders may at various times assume any of the three archetypal styles. Aquarian leader archetypes, like Buddha and Christ, flourished in the Arian and Piscean Ages respectively. A Piscean leader archetype like Mohammad displayed characteristics more often associated with the Arian leader archetype, such as the pursuit of the *Jihad*. An Aquarian leader archetype may resort to Arian leader archetype behavior, as did Abraham Lincoln during the American Civil War.

The Inspirational Leader understands the difference between Arian, Piscean, and Aquarian power. More importantly, Inspirational Leaders practice the generosity implied in Aquarian power and assume their true role as loving teachers, coaches, and spiritual guides to those they lead. Their aim is not to control others, but to liberate the greatness that is naturally within them. The Aquarian leader archetype is a giving leader, not a grasping one.

Aaron Feuerstein: Aquarian Leader

Aaron Feuerstein's grandfather founded Malden Mills in 1906. Located in Methuen and Lawrence, Massachusetts, Malden Mills is the largest maker of Polartec©, an outerwear fleece made of recycled plastic bottles.

Late on the bitterly cold night of December 11, 1995, Aaron Feuerstein raced from his seventieth-birthday party to the site of the inferno sweeping through the nineteenth-century mill buildings of his textile company. Three buildings burned to the ground, injuring thirty-three employees, eight of them very seriously. Many Malden Mills' employees rushed to the fiery scene, among them Michael Lavallee, an engineer, who couldn't believe his eyes. He imagined 3,100 high-paying textile jobs fading in the flames. "We just kept staring at the place, saying, 'It's over. It's done. It's gone.'"

Aaron Feuerstein saw it differently. Standing transfixed in the parking lot with other shaken employees and watching the sixty-mile-an-hour winds fan the flames, he vowed, "This is not the end." The conflagration tore through all of the buildings, except one warehouse that was the Polartec finishing plant. If that building stood, Feuerstein mused to an engineering executive standing beside him, the mill could continue production. The executive shook his head in amazement as he looked at Feuerstein. "You're always dreaming, Aaron," he said.

The Feuerstein family's strong spiritual beliefs have always guided their leadership practice. Feuerstein believes that manufacturers who stress high quality and commitment to people can win out over those who migrate to cheap labor. "People count!" is his simple philosophy. Bob Fawcett, Malden's director of corporate security and fire protection, described Feuerstein's reaction to the disaster: "There was no hesitation in his voice. He's always been a man of his word, and everyone believed him. We all shifted gears and said, 'Let's get going.'" William Piddick, a thirty-five-year Malden Mills veteran said, "You can't beat Aaron Feuerstein. I figured they wouldn't give up that easy."

Within twenty-four hours, Aaron Feuerstein delivered a message of hope to the employees who packed the gymnasium of the Central Catholic High School in Lawrence, Massachusetts. Grim-faced, he promised to rebuild the mill. As employees cheered, wept, and stood with their mouths open in grateful awe, Feuerstein went on to promise them a better Christmas than they had dared to hope for. He pledged to pay all employees for at least a month, and maintain their medical coverage, while he and his team developed a recovery plan. Later, this became a permanent commitment, costing $10 million. Not one employee was laid off because of the fire.

Feuerstein borrowed heavily from local banks to stay afloat and wangled the financing needed to rebuild his plant around a surviving clock tower long before he knew whether the $300 million would be covered by insurance. In the end, it all was. Charles K. Gifford, CEO of BankBoston, decided to become the lead lender in the $140-million financing package, because of Feuerstein's long history of high integrity and a relationship with the firm dating back to 1906. Integrity is a consistent pattern for Feuerstein. In 1981, Feuerstein had a brush with bankruptcy. Though it might have been simpler to walk away from a bankrupt textile mill in a three-hundred-year-old mill town, Feuerstein started again, paying wages that are 50 to 60% more than factories doing the same work, with a new mill and new products — Polartec and Polarfleece.

Feuerstein's decisions in the fire, as before, were based on his values. "At the time we did it," he said, "we did it because it was the right thing.

We didn't even consider business consequences." Many executives would have made the decisions differently. Observed local Senator Martin Meehan, "Feuerstein showed the difference when you have someone passionately committed to his workers. It would have been easier for him to retire." Meehan demonstrated his point by contrasting Feuerstein with Borden Foods Inc., in Columbus, Ohio, which had thrown five hundred employees out of work when it closed a spaghetti plant in Lowell. Practicing integrity that inspires others is deep within the Feuerstein philosophy. Malden helps employees to purchase their homes, thus enabling them to gradually rebuild deteriorating neighborhoods. Practices like these have helped Malden Mills become the largest employer in Lawrence and inspired many of its residents to name their children after Feuerstein.

"Fifty years ago, nothing would have been thought about somebody who rebuilt his factory after it had burned, who worried about his people and his community," says Feuerstein. "Today, a nerve has been struck, shocking people into the realization that the country is going in the wrong direction. ...chief executive officers, because of short-term gains, are cutting and killing off the very labor this country needs for its future."

Before the fire, state-of-the-art equipment had been delivered for installation in the factories that were now smoldering. This was unloaded from the trucks that had delivered them and installed in the spared facility. Within ten days, production was restarted. "Before the fire," Feuerstein said, "that plant produced 130,000 yards a week. A few weeks after the fire, it was up to 230,000 yards. Our people became very creative." Soon, sales of Polartec were ahead of pre-inferno levels. Idalinda Henriquez was not part of the team that was called back to work immediately after the fire, but she came back on her own anyway to pitch in anywhere she was needed. She describes her passion for this leader, who inspires her: "I wanted to show appreciation to Aaron Feuerstein. He's a good man. I'm a good worker. He needed our help."

Contrary to popular convention, good guys do win. One part of the business that couldn't be saved was the plant that produced flock, a synthetic velvet used in furniture, which accounted for $120 million of Malden's pre-fire sales. It was Malden's least profitable product, selling for $3 a yard, compared to $8 for Polartec. But tales of Feuerstein's integrity and Inspirational Leadership® have more than compensated for this loss, fueling demand for the higher-margin Polartec. Retailers such as L.L. Bean, Land's End, and Eddie Bauer regularly feature the brand name in their catalogs, making it one of the most recognized in the business. Customers remained loyal through the difficult reconstruction period, and employees stayed committed to the firm despite difficult staffing schedules. Letters of admiration poured into Feuerstein's office. One couple from Redwood, Washington, wrote, "We are seventy-two and retired and we spent our working lives hoping to find an employer with your moral stature." Enclosed were two one-dollar bills with a note that read, "In appreciation for what you are doing for your workers." Feuerstein leveraged his national status and recognition (President Clinton recognized Feuerstein in his 1995 State of the Union Address) with suppliers, customers, banks and insurers. New employees want to work in this fabled place, and with the new plant operating flawlessly, production is passing 900,000 yards of Polartec and Polarfleece each week, and sales will grow by more than 25%. "It's as if the heavens have opened up — just unbelievable," says Feuerstein.

Not really — it's just the magic that always happens around Aquarian leaders who serve their parceners.

Moving from Tired to Inspired

Lessons from a Young Inspirational Leader

In 1985, my friend Val Halamandaris founded the Caring Institute and the Hall of Fame for Caring Americans, to honor those who care for others with an award and to encourage the dissemination of caring values. Each year, eleven winners are selected from thousands of nominations to receive this prestigious award. What really characterizes these remarkable people is not their motivation, but their inspiration. Their power comes from within, not from any rewards that others might bestow from outside.

One of the winners in 1998 was twelve-year-old Jason Crowe, from Newburgh, Indiana. Saddened by the loss of his grandmother when he was ten, Jason created a neighborhood newspaper "by kids and for kids" in her memory. His paper, *The Informer,* now counts readers in twenty-five states, Washington, D.C., and four foreign countries. Children from around the world send Jason stories, drawings, puzzles, jokes, video game tips, and topics that appeal to children. Jason donates half the proceeds to the American Cancer Society. Thus, his paper provides much-needed funds for cancer research, while also helping to improve the self-esteem of children, as well as their awareness of a world beyond their communities.

In January, 1997, Jason read about the 1992 Sarajevo Breadline Massacre, in which a falling mortar shell killed twenty-two innocent men, women and children as they waited in line for food. Jason was moved by the response of Vedran Smailovic, principal cellist with the Sarajevo Opera Company, who witnessed the massacre from his apartment window and decided to act. Ignoring the continuing danger of the war raging around him, Smailovic sat in the exact place where the victims died and played his cello for twenty-two consecutive days in their honor. He became known as the "Cellist of Sarajevo." Jason was moved to share the story of Smailovic's heroism and compassion, and by doing so, showed the world how caring and service are achieved one person at a time, starting with oneself. Jason is raising money to create a statue of the "Cellist of Sarajevo" to be built and shipped to the people of Bosnia as a gift from America. President Clinton, musician Pete Seeger, singer Joan Baez, and cellist Yo-Yo Ma are supporting his efforts, and he has been invited to visit Sarajevo by the vice-president of Bosnia.

Confusing Motivation with Inspiration

We have been confusing *motivation* with *inspiration*. The dictionary tells us that to motivate is "to provide a motive; to induce, incite, impel" — something we *do to* people. We hire "motivational speakers" at conferences to "rev up the troops" and buy motivational posters, mugs, plaques, T-shirts, and greeting cards with messages such as "All the little things you've done make a BIG difference." Some people even create computer databases containing all of the birthdates of their friends, colleagues, and customers so that they can "surprise" them with their greetings on the appropriate day. Unfortunately, our levels of cynicism have reached epic proportions because we understand the technology of motivation, and we sometimes experience the hypocrisy of it. *Forbes* magazine reflected this sense of cynicism by proposing these tongue-in-cheek suggestions:

> *Maybe a poster for the boss's wall: "Thanks for all the overtime. I haven't seen my kids in years." Or a plaque: "This award is presented to [name of boss] for forcing me to make a BIG deference." For the factotum just forced out: A preprinted greeting card that says, "Here's to the day when the board does to you what you just did to me."*[21]

Motivation, which has been such an important part of the modern leader's toolkit, is a human resource "technique," a means for altering the behavior of others; in other words, it is a means of exploiting, controlling, and manipulating them. It is a self-focused practice too. When we attempt to motivate others, we intend to cause behavior in them that achieves something *we* want. When we attempt to motivate, we are not usually intending to serve others in their best interests. At its best, motivation is an attempt to serve others in *our* best interests. It is this transparently selfish intent that has caused such widespread cynicism in so many parceners today.

When we are motivated, our emotions and behavior are determined by external powers. When we are inspired, our emotions and behaviors are determined by powers from within. Many leaders have become adept at manipulating the personality — motivating people — but we have much to learn about inspiring the souls of parceners. Most leaders can't even bring themselves to talk this kind of language at work, fearing that they may appear foolish or distracted from the mission or the "key priorities of the organization." Yet, inspiration is the single most important need of parceners. Where people may be motivated to achieve, avarice and self-indulgence are the energies that propel them. The energy that propels inspiration is love. Motivation is self-focused; inspiration is other-focused. Motivation serves *me*; inspiration serves *you*. The difference in organizations is palpable. Inspired people arouse the hearts of others — thus creating inspired colleagues, customers, and suppliers — and an inspired world.

We can design incentive programs that will motivate; we can even motivate with fear. This is a common practice among many old story leaders because motivation exploits different levels of power — the power of one to punish or reward another. Motivation is therefore the currency of the Arian and Piscean leader archetypes.

Inspiration is strikingly different from motivation. The word is derived from the Latin root: *spirare,* meaning "spirit," to breathe, to give life, the breath of God. The dictionary defines inspiration as "breathing in, as in air to the lungs; to infuse with an encouraging or exalting influence; to animate; stimulation by a divinity, a genius, an idea or a passion; a divine influence upon human beings." It is not difficult to see the difference between "being motivated" and the blissful experience of inspiration. Motivation is a relationship between personalities; inspiration is a relationship between souls. Dennis Rodman is motivated; Michael Jordan is inspired. Val Halamandaris and Jason Crowe are inspired.

Inspiration does not depend on power relationships. On the contrary, when we are inspired, we are truly empowered. To inspire others, we must create an environment in which people sense a power beyond another human, a higher power, a divine influence that wells up from deep within, causing them to be infused with the breath of God. In other words, we must become as effective at engaging the energy of the soul (inspiration) as we have become in engaging the energy of the personality (motivation).

According to Watts Wacker, futurist with SRI International of Menlo Park, California, a culture is composed of five components. "One is a belief system. The second component is day-to-day existence and lifestyle. The third is how we communicate. The fourth component is how we treat other members of our species. The fifth is our orientation to spirituality. Belief systems are usually exclusionary, but orientations to spirituality are inclusionary. The founding fathers saw God as a clockmaker who made the clock, wound it up, brought it down here, and left. I would argue we may be moving to something more akin to God as co-conspirator, which would be a fundamental change in orientation to spirituality," says Wacker. And just who is this God as co-conspirator? "It's the God within you. It's turning your life over to a higher power, but recognizing that higher power lives within you," he says.[22]

Because we are so absorbed with perfecting the techniques of motivation, we feel compelled to "drive" everything. We overuse the word "driven." We want to be values-driven, customer-driven, market-driven, technology-driven, solutions-driven, and self-driven. Perhaps this is why so many people are driven to drink, driven insane, or driven to distraction. Are Zen masters "driven"? Is being driven not perhaps part of the problem rather than part of the solution? What would it look like if we were self-inspired? Or market-inspired? Or values-inspired? Would we prefer to be driven or inspired? I believe there is a greater sacredness and inner beauty associated with inspiration, the breath of God, compared to the manic style of our times, which causes us to be driven — and thus drained. We yearn to move from feeling tired to inspired.

Inspiration is that moment when we access the ineffable experience of the spirit inside us, which is the spirit that is one with the Universe. It is our muse, our creative juice, our love and passion and joy bursting from our heart in a tide of beautiful energy. Inspiration is an inner knowing that transcends any external motivation. Inspiration is thus a different class of experience from motivation.

The Dangers of Measuring the Ineffable

What makes the subject of inspiration such a difficult concept for Arian and Piscean leader archetypes to grasp is that, unlike motivation, we cannot measure it with the tools of management science. We can easily gauge the achievement of sales figures, budgets, finishing lines, and political campaigns. It is less easy to create the metrics for happiness, joy, beauty, love, loyalty, truth, dignity, respect, or bliss. The question we need to ask about analysis is, "Does it matter?" Why do we feel so compelled to measure everything? Why are the greatest and most inspiring events and experiences of humanity immeasurable by conventional, "scientific" means? Is it that only the mundane and nothing truly great yields to measurement?

Re-engineering the Orchestra

✓ Why do we need so many strings, when, with a little amplification, we could get by with eight or ten?

✓ Why not use those new five-string violins and eliminate the viola section altogether?

✓ Is it really necessary to pay the piccolo and bass trombone players for a whole night, when they only play about ten minutes' worth of music?

✓ Because the conductor doesn't make any musical sounds, could not several orchestras share the same conductor through large-screen video conferencing?

Source: Edmund H. Weiss, Fordham University Graduate School of Business

---

Anyone who says you can't see a thought doesn't know art.

WYNETKA ANN REYNOLDS

In the movie, *Dead Poet's Society*, Robin Williams plays the part of John Keating, the newly appointed English teacher at a private boys' school. In his first English class, he invites one of his students to read from a book entitled *Understanding Poetry*, by Dr. J. Evans Pritchard. The student describes the theories of Dr. Pritchard, who asserts that one may evaluate poetry with the use of a matrix, with "perfection" being measured on the vertical scale and "importance" on the horizontal, the total area being equal to "greatness." Thus, a poem by Byron, Pritchard suggests, might rate highly on the vertical, but poorly on the horizontal, while a Shakespearean sonnet might rate highly on both the vertical and the horizontal. When the student finishes, Keating turns to his class and exclaims, "Excrement! That's what I think of Dr. J. Evans Pritchard! We're not laying pipe — we're talking about poetry. How can you describe poetry like *American Bandstand* — 'Oh, I like Byron, I'll give him a 42, but I can't dance to it'?" To the amazement of his entire class, he underscores his view by asking them to rip out the chapter from their poetry textbook containing Dr. J. Evans Pritchard's theories, and toss it in the wastepaper basket. The startled students complete this ritual as Keating warns them of the dangers of measuring the unmeasurable in life. "The casualties could be your hearts and souls," he exclaims. "Armies of academics going forward measuring poetry! No! We'll not have that here... Now in my class, you will learn to think for yourselves again; you will learn to savor words and language. No matter what anyone tells you, words and ideas *can* change the world." Suspecting that some of his students believe that nineteenth-century literature has nothing to do with completing business or medical school, Keating continues, "We don't read and write poetry because it's cute, we read and write poetry because we are members of the human race, and the human race is filled with passion. Medicine, law, business, engineering — these are noble pursuits, and necessary to sustain life. But poetry, beauty, romance, love — these are what we stay alive for." Then, borrowing from Walt Whitman, Keating points out, "You are here, that life exists ... that the powerful play goes on, and you may contribute a verse." Peering intently into the faces of each student, he asks them, "And what will your verse be?"

We need to understand that there are some things that simply cannot be measured by conventional management metrics. How do you measure the smell of a baby, the beauty of the Mona Lisa, or the rush of a Rocky Mountain high? We long for heightened spiritual experiences in our working life. Inspiration of the soul goes beyond motivation and mathematics, and though we are forced by convention to reduce many things to a bar chart, resisting the temptation to always do so can inspire the soul. Inspirational Leaders know how to find fresh, instinctive, emotional, visceral measures to gauge our level of connectedness with the Universe at work.

Inspiration is often simply unexplainable. This, of course, is very unhelpful and frustrating for analysts so anxious to reduce leadership to a finite science made of quantifiable parts. But some things just *are*, their energy emanating from an inspired place. Sometimes, our inquiring scientific minds are not up to the task of analysis, and in those situations, it is best if we simply trust the divine. A four-kilometer-wide corridor separating North and South Korea, known as the Demilitarized Zone (DMZ), has been a no-go zone for people since it was mined and rimmed with razor wire at the end of the Korean War in 1953. South of the DMZ in South Korea, economic development has helped to extinguish all mammals larger than a mouse. But within the DMZ, where people do not tread for fear of becoming extinct themselves, leopards, tigers, and many endangered plants thrive and diversify. Divine intervention has not been intimidated by the evil motivations of people, and where people have banished themselves, numinous inspiration has prevailed for the other life with which we share our planet.

The buildings destroyed in Hiroshima by nuclear bombs were built from bricks formed from the clays of the mountains above. The dormant seeds of trumpet flowers captured in these building materials were released by the clash of atoms, and out of the ensuing rubble sprouted floral beauty. In Canada, the Jack Pine can only release its seeds when the heat of a forest fire opens its cones, thus enabling the seeds to fall on fertile soil. The acorn is an example of inspiration — inside rests the beauty of a majestic oak tree, waiting to be unlocked by love. Inspiration occurs in all of life and is measured in different ways than motivation. Inspiration is as natural to humans as motivation, and both are an essential part of our whole. Motivation is the *yang*; inspiration is the *yin*. The root of motivation can be found in the *personality*; the root of inspiration is to be found in the *soul*.

Inspired people become enthused. The word enthusiasm derives from the root words meaning to be inspired and being possessed by the divine. So enthusiasm means "one with the energy of God." Thus, inspiration and enthusiasm are conditions desired by us all. Individuals and teams who are inspired and enthused are operating in a different space/time continuum from the rest of us, and they know it, and relish it. Much to the chagrin of old story leaders, they frequently move from well-paying positions where they are highly motivated to lesser-paying positions where they are inspired. The new reality (although there is nothing really new about it, we have just been slow on the uptake) is that people want to work in inspiring organizations, for inspiring leaders, in inspiring industries and careers, doing work that inspires customers and suppliers and each other.

Anything less than this is just a job.

PART TWO

BECOMING AN INSPIRATIONAL LEADER

After speaking at a conference recently, I met a wise soul named Lin Teagle, who shared her philosophy of life with me:

**If you want something you've never had,
you have to do something you've never done.**

This sage advice can serve as the touchstone for the rest of this book. We want something better and different at work and, for that matter, in the rest of our lives. We yearn to reawaken spirit and values. Yet, there are no rules for Inspirational Leadership® because rules limit the response of the leader. The immune system has no rules; it mutates and responds to the changing environment. The Aquarian leader is guided the same way: to respond and adapt to meet the needs of the souls of others, because there are no others: we are one. Thus, when we inspire others, we inspire ourselves. This is why we all yearn to be inspired. The following chapters define the practice of Inspirational Leadership®. The complete model of the steps looks like this...

1. Defining the Leader's Uniqueness that Calls to Be Lived —
   The Destiny
2. Defining the Cause — a Magnet for Passion
3. Enabling Parceners to Find Their Calling
4. Aligning Calling and Cause
5. Serving Parceners
6. Guiding the Contribution of Brilliance
7. Creating the Environment that Encourages Parceners to Inspire
   Their Leader

Every communication between humans and other living things is an opportunity to inspire. Leadership is no exception. We are on this planet for a short time — this in itself is an inspiration. We should do nothing that spoils this magic or violates this divine trust. If notable military leaders can inspire their parceners to forfeit their lives in acts of extreme human sacrifice, violence and folly, we should have no excuse, nor difficulty, in inspiring others to a far higher bliss through love and grace.

Laying out the path for this journey, to learn the practices of the Inspirational Leader, is the purpose of the rest of this book.

Step One
Defining Our Destiny

The Path with a Heart

Anything is one of a million paths. Therefore you must always keep in mind that a path is only a path; if you feel you should not follow it, you must not stay with it under any conditions. To have such clarity you must lead a disciplined life. Only then will you know that any path is only a path, and there is no affront, to oneself or to others, in dropping it if that is what your heart tells you to do. But your decision to keep on the path or to leave it must be free of fear or ambition. I warn you. Look at every path closely and deliberately. Try it as many times as you think necessary. This question is one that only a very old man asks. My benefactor told me about it once when I was young, and my blood was too vigorous for me to understand it. Now I do understand it. I will tell you what it is: Does this path have a heart? All paths are the same: they lead nowhere. They are paths going through the bush, or into the bush. In my own life I could say I have traversed long, long paths, but I am not anywhere. My benefactor's question has meaning now. Does this path have a heart? If it does, the path is good; if it doesn't, it is of no use. Both paths lead nowhere; but one has a heart, the other doesn't. One makes for a joyful journey; as long as you follow it, you are one with it. The other will make your curse your life. One makes you strong; the other weakens you.

...the path without a heart will turn against men and destroy them. It does not take much to die, and to seek death is to seek nothing.

(For me there is only the travelling on paths that have heart, on any path that may have heart. There I travel, and the only worthwhile challenge is to traverse its full length. And there I travel looking, looking, breathlessly.)

Don Juan, *The Teachings of Don Juan: A Yacqui Way of Knowledge,*
Carlos Castaneda

**One must not always think
so much about what one
should do, but rather what
one should be. Our works
do not ennoble us; but we
must ennoble our works.**

MEISTER ECKHART

(*WORK AND BEING*)

A leader must feel inspired before they can inspire. This singular inspiration comes from a clear knowing about one's Destiny, the reason for being on this planet, the way we are connected on our journey with each other and the Universe. Few leaders know their purpose and mission in life — their Destiny — the uniqueness within them that calls to be lived. No leader can be great nor has earned the right to lead until they understand their Destiny, their higher purpose. The first step of Inspirational Leadership® therefore, is to **identify one's Destiny — our uniqueness within that calls to be lived.**

Destiny Is Authenticity

Aquarian leaders have an intimate relationship with their inner purpose and the path that inspires them. Until we have clearly identified, and are then following, our own destinies, we cannot be authentic leaders and help others to identify and follow their own true Destiny. As Max du Pree, former chairman of Herman Miller, observed, it is more important to reach our potential than to reach our goals.

Some, like Bill George, have always known their Destiny. Says George, "I have felt since I was a teenager that I had a calling to work in the business world in a leadership position where I could influence others to work to a high code of ethics. It took a while to find a place where I could find a near perfect match between mine and the company's values. Here at Medtronic, I feel I can really make a difference."

What is our purpose on this earthly journey? What is the uniqueness within us that calls out to be lived? This is the important starting point for us all. Most of us will die with our music still within us because, though we are given pure clarity at birth, society slowly clutters our inner awareness with its rules. And so we squeeze ourselves into the cookie-cutter molds that society deems to be best for us. As long as we are deaf to our intuition, our inner voice seeking to be heard, our true Destiny will go unrealized, and the music within us will remain unplayed.

Inspirational Leader Caroline Martin, Executive Vice President of Riverside Health System in Newport News, Virginia, described her Destiny to me this way:

"One way to live the belief 'if you believe it, you can see it,' in organizations is to give language to what you call a Cause. By using a common language, to paint word pictures of the yet unborn creation, others can see, believe it, add to it, and make it better.

My Cause happens to be transforming a sick-care delivery system into a well-care delivery system. That means, defining health to mean more than the absence of illness, determining who can have the greatest impact on facilitating health, and providing those services and products to folks if they don't already exist. But we must be able to articulate this, give words and definitions to health, body, mind, and spirit. To create a team or critical mass of like thinkers, the process must be fun, rewarding, and purposeful to work for, for members to invest in a Cause that may seem 'far out' or impossible. People must be allowed to play with the ideas and be encouraged to help in their development. We must affirm an idea before it's an actuality so that it can become an actuality.

> It is only with your heart that you can see rightly; what is essential is invisible to the eye.
>
> ANTOINE DE SAINT-EXUPÉRY

My objective at work is to create an environment where energy can manifest itself for a common Cause. I share an ideal (or hear and share someone else's ideal). Others build on it, and it becomes more beautiful than any of us imagined it could be. It means helping others operate from their strengths so they can enjoy being a part of something bigger than themselves."

We are each called to follow a specific journey, and for as long as we ignore or dishonor that call, we remain inauthentic. For some, because this pattern endures over a lifetime, life's lessons remain unlearned. They will be asked to learn them again. As long as we do not heed our inner voices, we remain untrue to ourselves, for we each have a uniqueness within that is calling to be heard — and lived.

> Keep away from people who try to belittle your ambitions. Small people always do that, but the really great make you feel that you too can become great.
>
> MARK TWAIN

Some hear the call, but are distracted by the mundane commitments of their current lives. In other cases, the messages are heard clearly, but must be tested. During my early career, I quickly became an executive with a very successful organization while still only in my mid-twenties. The years passed, and by many measures I was thriving, but in others I was somehow incomplete and restless. Some years earlier, I had read *My Life in*

Court by Louis Nizer, the famous American trial lawyer, and it had nourished my desire to become a criminal lawyer. My wife, who was raising our family, and my oldest daughter, who was finishing high school, urged me to quit and study law. They developed a plan — they would both go to work so that I could quit my lucrative executive position and go to law school. Presented with the opportunity and the loving support of my family, I had the chance to realize my dreams — to bring greater justice to the world. But when it came time to act on my dreams — I did not pursue a career in law, because I was not being called from within by a voice that cheered.

The important thing is to always listen and to discriminate — there is just one Destiny for each of us — just the uniqueness that yearns to be lived.

The Awakening

I am certain that after the dust of centuries has passed over our cities, we, too, will be remembered not for victories or defeats in battle or in politics, but for our contribution to the human spirit.

JOHN FITZGERALD KENNEDY

One day, a sudden storm arrives — illness or loss of job, loved one, or relationship — and we are shocked when our comfortable structures are torn away. In the new starkness, we become aware that we have been drifting for years. This brings an awakening. We realize that after all this time, we really have no idea where we are, how we got there, where we are going, or the purpose of our journey. Dante described the situation: "In the middle of the journey of our life I came to see myself in a dark wood where the straight way was lost." Many of us blindly follow a path with no passion — we simply slip onto a moving walkway, like the one at the airport, which streams us along with the rest of the harried and hurried crowd. We ask no questions — we tread the walkway, because everyone else does. We have no idea whether we are making a difference, creating happiness (for ourselves as well as others) or leaving a legacy. We sense a lack of connection to the Universe, an absence of enchantment and bliss in our lives, and we realize that there must be more.

These moments of awakening happen in different ways for different people. Some have always been aware of their uniqueness and have lived it all their lives, thus fulfilling their Destiny. Others never become enlightened this way. Many are brought face-to-face with the challenge of identifying their Destiny somewhere during the unfoldment of their lives. Whether it is in a moment of crisis or in a routine reassessment of our life's path, we will be invited to pause and ask ourselves the question, "What is my Destiny?" When we ask this question, by implication we are also asking the great question of Perceval from the Arthurian legend: "Whom does it serve?" In the legend of King Arthur, the Holy Grail was known to reside in the castle of the Fisher King, and would remain there until a visitor, upon viewing it, would ask, "Whom does it serve?" Only the rightful owner of the Holy Grail would ask this question. When the great knight Perceval visited the castle, he failed to ask the question and thus failed to claim the Holy Grail. It is the same for us all. Until we first ask these and other questions, and then satisfactorily answer them, we are mere suggestions of our potential — flowers without a sun. This discovery and the resulting journey create the warmth that kindles the passion, which then leads to the definition of our personal vision, our Cause — no matter where we are in our lives.

It's Never Too Late

> **We are generally afraid to become that which we can glimpse in our most perfect moments.**
>
> ABRAHAM MASLOW

Many of the greatest leaders that have ever lived — Buddha, Christ, Mohammed, Jefferson, Martin Luther King, St. Francis, Mother Teresa — did not discover their Destiny until the latter parts of their lives. Christ was a carpenter for the first thirty years of His life — His greatness was compressed into the last *three* years of His life. St. Francis, the son of a prosperous merchant, took part in several military operations as a mercenary soldier before he felt himself called to be a preacher and mystic at the age of twenty-seven. He founded two holy orders in the last third of his life, dying when he was forty-five. Buddha was a wealthy prince, who did not begin his spiritual journey until he was twenty-nine, taking six more years before reaching enlightenment.

Bill Wilson was forty before he started the organization that would change the lives of millions — Alcoholics Anonymous. Rosa Parks was forty-two when she signaled the beginning of

> **One truth stands firm. All that happens in world history rests on something spiritual. If the spiritual is strong, it creates world history. If it is weak, it suffers world history.**
>
> ALBERT SCHWEITZER

the end of segregation and ushered in a new phase of the civil rights movement by refusing to give up her seat to a white passenger on a bus. Jim McCann spent fourteen years as a social worker at St. John's Home for Boys in Rockaway, New York, before becoming the Inspirational Leader who transformed a company teetering on the edge of bankruptcy into a $300-million success called 1-800-FLOWERS. Tom Block went the other way. As CEO of H & R Block Inc., the world's largest tax preparation company, he took a 98% pay cut from his $618,000 annual salary to teach math at a Kansas City Catholic school of mostly minority students. As these examples attest, there is no right time in our lives to discover our uniqueness that calls to be lived. The timing is unimportant. What is important is that we discover our true Destiny, and thus become authentic, before we can grow into an Inspirational Leader. These discoveries by many leaders late in their lives serve as a beacon for each of us as we struggle to define our own journeys. It is never too late.

Cal Turner: Inspirational Leader

I first met Cal Turner when I was speaking at Vanderbilt University in Nashville, Tennessee. As chairman of Dollar General Stores, Cal is one of the school's largest benefactors. We hit it off immediately, and I fell in love with this wonderful man whose big heart, large vision, noble values, and spiritual underpinnings have created a retailing phenomenon. Founded by Cal's father, Dollar General sells low-cost merchandise in stores located in poorer neighborhoods across the United States — the areas other retailers avoid. Under Cal's Inspirational Leadership® of 27,400 parceners (he calls them partners) the firm became a Fortune 500 company in 1999 for the first time with sales of $3.2 billion (a blistering increase of 23% over the prior year).

How did Cal Turner discover his Destiny?

I had the hell scared out of me; I was scared to be called into the ministry. A minister said to me, "Cal, I'll give you some advice about the ministry: Don't do it." There are many in the ministry who are not called to be in it. I believe you have to find what it is you want to do, and do it.

One of my life's greatest challenges was being the boss' son. I could never be fully independent, being fearful of how I could keep such an organization going. I decided to develop professional management, and hang on to the entrepreneurial past of the company. I knew I didn't know much about retailing myself.

I would try to recruit partners from our customers; we would develop talent from our customer base. This helped us to become number one. I really went into the business of ministry. This is the ministry. The culture and people of this business are like rising water lifting my boat. I'm not very smart; I've never run a store; I'm not a buyer because I'm gullible; I don't even understand this business. I just ask the questions, and get answers.

One of the side benefits of Inspirational Leadership® is that it works. The Cause of Dollar General Stores is "Fun stores where true partners give customers a better life." Cal Turner is a missionary creating a highly successful commercial enterprise *and* a ministry — in fact they are the same thing. Cal knows you need both profits and noble values — that is the essence of his Destiny. He says, "I think others will get more turned onto values if they see a real-world demonstration of the positive impact of those values. We demonstrate this — ours are 'wow' numbers. Values are the basis for the 'wow.' Big values create big numbers."

Dollar General Corporation
Serving Others!

• A Better Life... for our customers

• A Superior Investment... for our shareholders

• A Partnership in Total Development... with our employees

How does this work? Cal describes a particular aspect of his business ministry:

> Our company has an inner city initiative for ministering to the neighborhood. We put a store and a classroom in the neighborhood, and sell merchandise at lower prices than those that can be found anywhere else in the country. Neighboring retailers jack up prices to cover for theft, etc., but we don't need to — our stores are profitable. We sell bleach, cleaning products, men's and ladies' clothing, vitamins, toys, and stationery at very reasonable prices. We have an economic ministry. The students in the classroom spend half the day working and half the day in school. They have all been on welfare, and this is their first work experience. Working in the store enhances the classroom experience. To date, we have helped to get six hundred people off welfare through this program.

> Our initiative involves many partners. These are the true down-and-out potential customers of our company. I went to a graduation ceremony,

and one graduate said to me, "Thanks to your store, I have been drug-free for five months, and so have my kids. 'Just say no' don't get it, when their mama was swallowing it, punching it, poking it. Now, don't you claim too much, Mr. Turner — the Lord Jesus is responsible for this, but he could not get to me until I was in your store." How do you compute the ROI of the store when this one person and her family have the opportunity to be drug-free? What is a life worth in the financial gain of ROI?

Many can't bridge the gap when the standards of employment are getting higher due to technology. We decided to take what we do — operate stores — and help the community. Our entry-level employment is at minimum wage. They must be paid $8 per hour to break even and get off government support. Getting these people off welfare may be idealistic, but we now know six hundred people who are.

I want the world to know — I want leaders in all organizations to be challenged to consider what organizations can do, and the leveraging of activities to benefit society. Here's how I see it:

Store + classroom = off welfare.

These people who are on welfare need many resources to get off. They need childcare; we arrange for childcare to be provided by outside partners who are close to the store. The persons who run the program must be carefully selected. Normally they need transportation — but we reversed the situation — we brought the classroom-store to them!

These clients have never been employed; if they don't show up, the people running the programs go and knock on their doors, wake them up, get them up, and bring them in. They need counseling in many areas, including basic hygiene, how to dress, why they should show up on time, transportation to job interviews, transportation to their jobs, and how to present themselves in a job interview.

When a store was torched recently and a white policeman killed an African-American, a riot ensued. The community of Nashville was up in arms; what to do divided the whole community. Our customers resented what they felt to be police abuse, while the well-to-do of Nashville resented the down and out for burning the store.

Amid this tension, we rebuilt the store even though we had inadequate insurance proceeds. The classrooms were bigger, we provided a laundromat to avoid our customers' clothes being stolen while they were hanging out to dry. Contractors donated materials. The downtown Rotary Club and many other organizations provided a labor of volunteers. There was a community-wide clean-up day. Altogether three hundred volunteers from across Nashville pitched in to help us rebuild the store. The whole community was involved in this demonstration of friendship.

Cal Turner creates light for others to blaze the trail. He has found his Destiny, which is to create a successful business and a successful business ministry.

Jerry Chamales: Inspirational Leader

In the 1970s, Scotch and cocaine supplied Jerry Chamales' highest moments. At the tender age of twenty-seven, Chamales was, he says, "at the bottom of the food chain, bent like a pretzel." After Chamales dried out and straightened up his life, he founded Omni Computer products in Carson, California, which has since grown into a $30-million producer and remanufacturer of computer supplies and recycled printer cartridges. Chamales has found his Destiny and is living it through his company — one-third of Omni's 270 employees are, like him, formerly workless or homeless, drug addicts or alcoholics. Many are ex-convicts. Chamales recruits many of his employees at halfway houses, work-furlough centers, and recovery programs. He then assigns a mentor and puts them through a rehabilitation program sponsored by Omni. Chamales posts bail when his employees brush with the law, attends recovery programs with new hires and maintains a close relationship with a bondsman, who puts him in touch with prospective employees. One employee worked for Omni for eighteen months, but repeatedly fell off the wagon. After enrolling in a recovery program, he joined another company like Omni, being too ashamed to return. But Joe Hiller, himself a former addict and now Omni's vice-president of sales, came looking for him. "Why don't you come home?" Hiller asked the employee when he found him. Chamales is a successful businessman, but he is also a successful therapist and rehabilitation expert, and this has helped him to become a successful human being and Inspirational Leader.

> **You can't do anything about the length of your life, but you can do something about its width and depth.**
>
> SHIRA TEHRANI

Step Two

Defining the Cause

No vision and you perish
No ideal, and you're lost;
Your heart must ever cherish
Some faith at any cost.
Some hope, some dream to cling to,
Some rainbow in the sky,
Some melody to sing to,
Some service that is high.

— HARRIET DU AUTERMONT

Inspirational Leaders next identify and define their magnetic vision — their *Cause*, which flows directly from the pure clarity of their Destiny. **Inspirational Leaders then champion a Cause — a magnetic vision so powerful that it draws people and their passion to it from afar.** They feel called to contribute and add their energy, love, passion, and support to the Cause. The greatest leaders in history, Christ, Buddha, Gandhi, Martin Luther King, Thomas Jefferson among them, did not form a committee in order to achieve a "buy-in" to their vision. They didn't have to sell their ideas — their ideas were so powerful that people were drawn to them — their vision was a Cause. A Cause comes from within. It is not a committee thing.

The Cause

Your talent is the Creator's divine gift to you. What you do with it is your gift back to the Creator.

Let no one be discouraged by the belief there is nothing one man or woman can do against the enormous array of the world's ills — against misery and ignorance, injustice and violence.... Few will have the greatness to bend history itself, but each of us can work to change a small portion of events, and in the total of all those acts will be written the history of this generation....It is from numberless, diverse acts of courage and belief that human history is shaped.

Each time a person stands up for an ideal, or acts to improve the lot of others, or strikes out against injustice, he sends forth a tiny ripple of hope, and crossing each other from a million different centers of energy and daring, these ripples build a current that can sweep down the mightiest walls of oppression and resistance.

ROBERT F. KENNEDY

The greatest leaders in history all saw a beacon beckoning to them from the future — a Cause. They had a clear vision of the world they sought to create and a burning passion to bring that world into existence. For them, and for many others, their Cause defined a future world brightened by the light of their dream.

A Cause is a dream that connects us from our present reality to a richly imagined future. A compelling Cause makes the hairs on our neck stand up. It quickens our pulse and stirs our imagination. It excites us into action. A Cause is the spark that fuels the ideology that blossoms into a movement. It encourages us to fall in love with the present again because it paints a clear, magical, and uplifting picture of our chosen path to the future. A grand and compelling Cause ignites passion. In short, a compelling Cause is a covenant so powerful that it becomes a magnet that draws others to it, like pilgrims to a sacred shrine. It doesn't need to be "pitched" or hawked because it is so inherently sound, and this soundness is what naturally draws people to it. The appeal of a Cause is the profound and unique strength it holds. Think of the Kevin Costner character in the movie *A Field of Dreams*; his Cause was so powerful he knew that his mission was to "build it and they will come."

A magnetic Cause connects first with the Divine, the Universal Consciousness — and then works backwards to the reality of the present. A great Cause builds a bridge between the Divine and the temporal that captures the imagination of those who hear it. This is what draws parceners to a Cause.

Three animating features are present in the Cause of Inspirational Leaders:

1. The Cause is patient, embracing, and engaging with a long view.
2. The Cause seeks to ennoble others, not to enrich the visionary.
3. The Cause "channels" Inspirational Leaders for something greater than themselves or their actions.

In other words, the Inspirational Leader responds to a clear inner voice and thus becomes the spokesperson for a richly imagined future.

When Martin Luther King, Jr. delivered his famous speech in Washington, D.C., on August 28, 1963, to an audience of more than 200,000 civil rights supporters, he was deeply aware of the need for patience and holding the long view. He sought to ennoble people by proclaiming his Cause. He said, "I have a dream that one day this nation will rise up and live out the true meaning of its creed: 'We hold these truths to be self-evident, that all men are created equal.' ... I have a dream that my four little children will one day live in a nation where they will not be judged by the color of their skin but by the content of their character." It was a dream, not for next week, or next month, or even for next year, but forever in the future. This was, and still is, a Cause that inspires the hearts of millions of people, not just African-Americans, because it appeals to the souls of all people. King was speaking to the soul. It was outrageous and irrational, given the situation at the time, but even so, millions of people found it totally enthralling. We are all yearning for a heightened level of inspiration, and we will align ourselves with a great Cause and freely undergo untold hardships in order to help realize a dream that ignites our passion. King achieved this by defining a Cause that was divinely inspired, and far greater than himself — he spoke about an ideal, a future world that he could see in his heart, into which he was pouring his life and which came from a higher source — and millions could identify with it and were drawn to his Cause.

> **Nothing happens unless first a dream.**
>
> CARL SANDBURG

A Cause Is Not a Corporate Mission Statement

A compelling Cause is characterized by two vital elements: it honors the sacredness of people, and it is the inspiration of one person. This stands in stark contrast to the tone and content of modern corporate mission statements. Most contemporary leaders believe in two myths: (1) corporate mis-

You see things and you say
"Why?"; but I dream things
that never were and I say
"Why not?"

GEORGE BERNARD SHAW

sion statements are the result of a team effort; and (2) corporate mission statements define quantifiable goals.

Historically, corporate mission statements have tended to be litanies directed at employees, shareholders, and customers, describing how the organization intends to become larger, stronger, more powerful, and dominant — statements flowing from Arian and Piscean leadership thinking. After a while, these earthly, egocentric visions all start to look alike. Shuffle the names and some of the clichés, and they are fully interchangeable. We can no longer afford small, self-serving missions. Small missions are already too commonplace, lackluster, and dispiriting. Goethe urged us to "dream big dreams." Robert Browning urged us to ensure that the reach of our dreams was just beyond our grasp.

Bill George of Medtronic puts it this way:

People must be motivated by a deeper cause. Our mission is not maximizing shareholder value. One of the things that I like to do is talk to shareholders about our mission. Recently, we were having a breakfast meeting with the board of directors of one of our largest shareholders. They had made a huge profit in the value of their shareholdings. They asked about Medtronic. I said that Medtronic is not in the business of maximizing shareholder value; that we are maximizing the value to patients, serving them well. Through serving patients, we are ultimately serving the shareholders well. One of the keys to our success is continuing to reinforce that. Medtronic is a mission-inspired company. We talk about the mission everyday. Every decision is made with the purpose to restore people to full life and health. Our mission is central and core to everything that the company does. It is a great motivator to our people. I believe that people don't come to work to earn money for themselves and the company. They come to work because the product does something worthwhile, and this is what gets people inspired.

What Bill George is talking about is the Cause of his company, crafted by the company's visionary founder Earl Bakken (inventor of the external pacemaker) in 1949. Not one word has been altered since. When new parceners join the company, Bill George gives each of them a mission card and a book describing the company. They watch a video about the founder, and Bill George tells anecdotal stories about how being at Medtronic has affected his life. "At the end of this, each employee comes up, and I give them a medallion that is three inches across and has a picture of a person rising because they have become well. On the back is part of the mission. I say to each of them, 'I ask in accepting this that you accept the mission of Medtronic and look at it and display it to remind you that the purpose of your being here is to restore people to full life and health. If you get frustrated, note that there is a higher Calling.'"

It is important to make this distinction between traditional corporate mission statements and a Cause, as we are using these terms. A mission usually tends to be defined in terms of *our* needs, whereas a Cause is *always* defined in terms of the needs of others — it defines how we intend to serve. Where a mission might say, "To be the best health system in America," a Cause would state, "To create the healthiest community in America." The Cause at St. Claire's Hospital in Schenectady, New York, is "We welcome life at its inception, and nurture it with love and understanding throughout its existence." Jeff Bezos, the founder of Amazon.com, might have created a mission such as "To be the dominant e-trader on the Internet." Instead it is "To be the world's most customer-centered company." A mission often draws its energy from the ego, describing the rewards we hope for when our mission is realized. A Cause draws its energy from the soul, describing the way we plan to honor the souls of others, how we will recognize their sacredness, improve their lives, and serve them. A mission is self-centered; a Cause is other-centered. A Cause creates passion because it describes passion. Although a mission may refer to the same future, a Cause inspires because it puts *others* — their personalities *and* their souls — first.

Hunter (Patch) Adams, the doctor whose fame grew when Robin Williams portrayed him in a movie very loosely based on his life, has a magnetic Cause. Adams plans to build the Gesundheit! Institute, a forty-room healthcare facility on 310 rural acres in Pocahontas County, West Virginia. The Institute will be a theme-park like, forty-bed healthcare facility that offers free healthcare to patients from anywhere in the world. A planned eye clinic will be shaped like an eyeball and a sewer treatment center shaped like a backside. Many physicians have been inspired by his vision of compassionate, humor-filled, patient-centered wellness programs. Without any advertising or recruitment, Adams has created a magnetic Cause that is so powerful, more than one thousand physicians have applied to work gratis at the Gesundheit! Institute when it eventually opens.

The Cause That Inspires

The first objective of a grand Cause is that it speaks — or more accurately sings, croons, cheers, and shouts — to the soul. It engages the heart and the mind. When others learn about a Cause, it makes such a complete connection with their minds, hearts, and souls, that they yearn to share the same vision, to experience the same passion and exhilaration and to invest their energy in the Cause that they now share. It is a visceral experience. A Cause speaks to our inner knowing, to our spirit, to something that is not of this world. A great Cause is not so much about the material as it is about the metaphysical. It is more about magic and mysticism than economics and efficiency. A Cause engages us at a level that is mystical, rising far above the mere details of goals and organizational targets.

Over the last quarter-century, The ServiceMaster Company has doubled its revenues every three and a half years and now enjoys system-wide revenues exceeding $6 billion. The ServiceMaster team of 240,000 people clean toilets and floors, maintain boilers and air-handling units, serve food, kill bugs, care for lawns and landscapes, clean carpets, provide maid service, and repair home appliances. The company has increased its profits every quarter for twenty-eight years, largely through innovation and offering new services — 75% of their revenues come from services new to the company's portfolio during the last ten years.

The chairman, C. William Pollard, describes why the company's Cause is the single most important contributing factor to his company's stellar performance.

"When you visit the headquarters of our firm located west of the city of Chicago, you walk into a large, two-story lobby, and on your right is a curving marble wall, ninety feet long and eighteen feet high. Carved in stone on that wall in letters eight feet high are four statements that constitute our [Cause]: To Honor God in All We Do, To Help People Develop, To Pursue Excellence, and To Grow Profitably. A statement simple enough to be remembered — controversial enough to raise questions requiring a continuous process of explaining and relating — and profound enough to be lasting. If you were to tour the rest of the building, you would notice that nearly all of the work spaces are moveable. Most of the walls do not reach to the ceiling. Practically everything in the building is changeable and adaptable, just like the marketplace we serve with its changing demands and opportunities. But the marble wall conveys a permanency

It is difficult to say what is impossible, for the dream of yesterday is the hope of today and the reality of tomorrow.

ROBERT H. GODDARD

that does not change. The principles carved in this stone are lasting. The first two objectives are end goals. The second two are means goals. As we seek to implement these objectives in the operation of our business, they provide for us a reference point for seeking to do that which is right and avoiding that which is wrong. They remind us that every person has been created in the image of God with dignity and worth and great potential. We do not use our first objective as a basis of exclusion. It is, in fact, the reason for our promotion of diversity, as we recognize that different people are all part of God's mix."

Because a Cause rises above the mundane, it enables us to see magic where others see problems. A Cause combines ideas together so that new realities are created. Above all, a Cause inspires because it is always rooted in love. A Cause is magnetic because it draws people to it and inspires them to rethink their options in creative ways that will manifest reality. A Cause may contain raw data and statistics, but more than anything, it is energized by passion and appeals to the spirit even more than the intellect.

The social object of skilled investment should be to defeat the dark forces of time and ignorance which envelop our future.

JOHN MAYNARD KEYNES

For example, a Cause might be *the eradication of extreme poverty in the world*. A Cause becomes magnetic when it contains a clear blueprint for implementation: The United Nations has estimated that the cost of eradicating extreme poverty in the world is $40 billion per year. This would provide the 1.3 billion souls who earn $1 per day or less with basic healthcare and nutrition (annual cost $13 billion), primary schooling ($6 billion), low-cost clean water and sanitation ($9 billion) and reproductive health and family planning ($12 billion). The total wealth of the top two hundred of the world's four hundred billionaires exceeds $1.3 *trillion* — more than the entire income of the poorest half of the world's population. During 1997, the assets of these two hundred richest people in the world grew by 30%, yet an asset allocation of only 3% would eradicate the world's extreme poverty. Only an absence of creative thinking on the part of the world's governments and their taxation and foreign aid policies stands in the way of this becoming a Cause, which if it did, would result in a phenomenal spiritual and material impact on the world. A recent World Bank study has revealed that investment in basic nutrition yields a fif-

Treat people you do business with as if they were part of your family. Prosperity depends on how much understanding one receives from the people with whom one conducts business.

KONOSUKE MATSUSHITA

If we cannot make a profit, that means we are committing a sort of crime against society. We take society's capital, we take their people, we take their materials, yet without a good profit, we are using precious resources that could be better used elsewhere.

KONOSUKE MATSUSHITA

teen-fold return in GNP growth.

The late Konosuke Matsushita built a globe-straddling business from scratch to $45 billion, employing 256,000 people. He has given the world names like Panasonic, Quasar, and National and, through thousands of innovations and patents, improved the lives of millions. Matsushita's beginnings were modest but inspired. Early in his career, he was invited by a client to the head temple of the Tenrikyo religious sect, and this had a profound effect on his life. He wrote later, "There was something to be learned from the way [the temple] was apparently thriving, from the mountains of donated logs, from the energetic and dedicated way the members of the sect threw themselves into the construction work." Matsushita reasoned that if a corporation were as meaningful as a spiritual practice, it would greatly benefit people. Two months later, on May 5, 1932, he unveiled his Cause to 168 office workers at the Osaka Central Electric Club. He began by reminding them of their impressive achievements: the company was only fifteen years old, but already employed 1,100 people, generated annual revenues of 3 million yen, owned 280 registered patents, and operated 10 factories. Then he made a proclamation: "The mission of a manufacturer should be to overcome poverty, to relieve society as a whole from misery, and bring it wealth." Using tap water as a metaphor because it is freely available to almost anyone, he continued, "This is what the entrepreneur and the manufacturer should aim at: to make all products as inexhaustible and as cheap as tap water. When this is realized, poverty will vanish from the earth." From this day on, the Cause of the company was aligned with important human values.[23]

Planning at Matsushita is established over a 250-year time span. Matsushita built a remarkable business without centralized structure, excessive bureaucracy, internal focus, high costs or slow response time, while embracing optimistic and ethical purposes, communicating these widely, and helping others to excel.

Human resources consultants William M. Mercer surveyed employees to determine if benefits, policies, and practices influenced them when choosing an employer or improving their personal productivity. Most of respondents (64%) said that a "clear sense of organizational purpose" would influence them more than almost all traditional employee benefits, except a retirement or savings plan and a pension plan.[24] The power of a Cause to attract people to an organization and its leader matches, and often exceeds, any material incentive.

> **If you have built castles in the air, your work need not be lost; that is where they should be. Now put the foundations under them.**
>
> HENRY DAVID THOREAU

More than just affairs of the head, great Causes are affairs of the heart. While the head may warn us that the new Cause is outrageous and irrational, the heart will tell us this doesn't matter. In fact, most compelling Causes may initially strike us as being intellectually outrageous — this is their appeal. The lasting magic of Aquarian leader archetypes, such as Martin Luther King or Gandhi, is the ringing passion of their Causes. When Martin Luther King gave his famous speech, he was speaking from the heart. In an earlier period when slavery was still common practice, who would have thought that the Quakers, William Lloyd Garrison, and the other leading abolitionists were making any sense? An important question for us to keep asking is, "Does it inspire the soul?"

Some years ago, I bought one of the first PalmPilots, those ubiquitous palm-sized computer organizers. It was one of the most liberating work-related things I had ever done. I reveled in the freedom it conferred. It seemed totally intuitive, requiring no user manual to get going — it felt like technology for the soul. The first day I owned it, I flew to Monterrey, California, to make a speech, and after checking into the hotel, I went for a walk at dusk along the surf's edge. After a few moments, I began to decompress from my travels. Without notice, my muse became hyperactive, and I felt compelled to jot down the ideas that were streaming in to my brain. I was able to take out my PalmPilot, turn it on, note my ideas in it, and continue my solo stroll caressed by the sea breezes.

Donna Dubinsky and Jeff Hawkins created the fabulously successful PalmPilot while they were at U.S. Robotics, later acquired by 3Com Inc. It was the fastest-selling computer product in technological history. Two years later, they left to start their own firm, Handspring. Venture capitalists, partners, and would-be collaborators lined up to follow their Cause — to make palm computing as accessible, particularly to children, as a wristwatch.

Causes come in all sizes, big and small. Mothers, department managers, priests, nurses, teachers, law enforcement officers, community leaders (a leader is anyone who inspires others) can craft a Cause that is so magnetic it draws people to their richly imagined future.

The Myths of "Buy-In" and "Shared Vision"

Unlike the old story model of leadership that calls for leaders to orchestrate a buy-in from the rest of the organization, Inspirational Leadership® calls for the Cause to be so compelling that organizing a "buy-in" is superfluous. If the Cause is so magnetic that it attracts parceners who are eager to support its aims, what need is there to orchestrate a buy-in? Coercing others to believe in a Cause amounts to tacitly transferring the responsibility for crafting and articulating the right Cause in the first place. If the Cause is inherently brilliant, it will attract legions of parceners; if it is a weak Cause, it will need to be sold to those parceners who are already members of the team. This is the difference between a brilliant Cause conceived by a visionary Inspirational Leader, and one designed by a committee. They are as different as a benediction from a blasphemy. We don't need buy-in; we need fire, passion, and ownership.

The Singular Vision

Another contemporary myth about vision-crafting is that it should be a shared idea, thus reducing the risk of others failing to buy in to it. As a consequence, visions that were once extraordinary are adapted, modified, and pummeled, until their fire and passion are squeezed out of them. These consensus visions reach for the *lowest* common denominator where an accord can be built — egalitarian and democratic, but soulless and lacking in magic. In other words, they suffer from a fatal flaw — compromise.

Let me tell you about the Cause of my own organization, The Secretan Center Inc. We are a worldwide virtual consulting organization, working with corporations, healthcare, education, law enforcement, and not-for-profit and governmental organizations. We have more than sixty certified Secretan Center Associates spanning Europe, North and South America, and Australia, who have completed an intensive learning program with us. These Associates teach and consult in partnership and independently with us, using our proprietary concepts and their own rich and diversified gifts. In addition, we have a growing worldwide family called The Higher Ground Community, numbering several hundreds, which is linked together in a global network, committed to changing the world by bringing greater spirituality and higher values to the workplace. We hold international conferences and retreats, run workshops and seminars, have formed local chapters, maintain a website (http://www.secretan.com), where there are several Internet discussion forums, and we have started a number of worldwide initiatives, including Spirit@Work Day. Our Cause is "To change the world by awakening spirit and values at work." We know that in order to make this world of ours work a little better, we must effect the changes we seek through the most powerful institutions on the planet — in the world of business. We also know that people want to be inspired and that this is achieved one person at a time, and that when a group of inspired people commits to reawakening spirit and values at work, they become an inspired team, and that groups of teams become an inspired community, and that an inspired world is simply the coming together of inspired communities. So we have defined our cause in this compact way:

> **All good work is done the way ants do things, little by little.**
> LAFCADIO HEARN

Inspired people. Inspired teams.
Inspired communities. Inspired world.

Of course, we all strive to be a living example of Inspirational Leadership®. Every day, people call, write and e-mail us inquiring about our work because they have been drawn to us by our Cause. This is one way we try to practice what we teach. As you will see elsewhere in this book, we attempt to practice all seven of the steps to Inspirational Leadership® — and like everyone else, we have our good and bad days. Our intent though, and we are mostly successful, leads to the inspiration of those with whom we come into contact.

The Courage to Speak Our Truth

In our role as leaders, we are the *role models for others,* and for this reason, we have a responsibility to inspire others by showing them our

**Words are, of
course, the most
powerful drug used
by mankind.**

RUDYARD KIPLING

courage and modeling the way by speaking our truth. We often disguise our words because we believe that people are not ready to hear the language of the spirit. How did the greatest Aquarian leaders of all time feel about this? Did Buddha disguise his language? Did he use camouflage words such as "caring" and "compassion," when he really meant love and grace, in order to avoid offending his audiences? Isn't this a test of our personal courage? If we can't even bring ourselves to say the words, how can we teach the ideas? If we fudge the language, we are probably less enlightened, or authentic, than those we lead and teach.

When we say that others are not ready to hear or use the language of spirituality at work, of Inspirational Leadership®, and that words like *love* and *soul* will not sit well with modern employees, we may be *projecting*.

Projection is a word coined by psychologists to describe a process whereby an individual projects onto another person certain denied, or shadow, behaviors or characteristics of his or her own personality. When a person is projecting, they attribute certain personal traits or feelings to someone else to protect their own ego from acknowledging that the same attributes actually exist within themselves. Individuals who have trouble getting along with others often project the difficulty onto others, perhaps perceiving acquaintances as being obnoxious, when the shortcoming is their own. Language touches our emotions, triggering our egos, and when we let our egos drive our language, we are trapped into projecting.

For many years, we have fooled ourselves into believing that the workplace is an inappropriate setting for emotions, spiritual language, or beliefs that demonstrate a profound respect and caring for humans. Often, this is a classic case of projection: the things we say that others are not yet ready for, are the things that *we* are not yet ready for. Thus, by projecting this way, we may be protecting our egos, but we are imprisoning our souls. When we do our inner work, we may discover that it is we who are not yet ready, not they. The truth is most of us have been intimidated by a secular society and an excess of political correctness that has forced us to hide our true feelings and needs. It is the most natural urge in the Universe for the spirit within us all to yearn for retrieval, to reclaim the lost spiritual dimensions

**It is hard to believe that
a man is telling the truth
when you know that you
would lie if you were in
his place.**

H.L. MENCKEN

of our working lives. Indeed it is the essential juice of life and to deny it is contrary to our very essence. What ails us in the workplace is the result of this denial and suppression. The resulting flow of toxic energy in the workplace alienates us even more from each other and from our work — and it saddens the soul.

The problem is that we have all succumbed to so many years of intimidation that we fear going first. But deep in every heart at work, we are all looking at each other and wondering, "Who will take the first step? Who will be the brave one? Who will lead? Who will say the words I want to hear?" As soon as we see someone else displaying compassion, love, and grace at work, the floodgates open, everyone pours through the breach and embraces the leader for their courage and authenticity. This is the role of the Aquarian leader archetype.

Jefferson's Compromise

If Thomas Jefferson had not bent to the pressures of his peers, he would have written the American Declaration of Independence (a Cause if ever there was one) quite differently, and it would have been necessary for Martin Luther King to search for different words for his famous speech. Jefferson originally penned the phrase "We hold these truths to be *sacred*, that all men are created equal, that they are endowed by their Creator with certain unalienable Rights, that among these are Life, Liberty and the pursuit of Happiness."

Sacred! Not "self-evident." This change, when compared to the original, has the feeling of great visionary work diluted by a committee. Benjamin Franklin convinced Jefferson to alter the words. How would history have been affected had the original intent of sacredness been retained? What might have happened if the Declaration of Independence had required that "Life, Liberty and the pursuit of Happiness" be considered *sacred*? How would it have affected our thinking, philosophy, and approaches to the world? If life were considered sacred today, would violence have become as prevalent as it has? How would sacredness have shaped our attitudes towards guns, war, prisons, poverty and crime? If liberty were considered *sacred*, would our levels of incarceration and recidivism still be among the highest in the world? What would Martin Luther King have said instead? Would King have needed to make the speech at all?

The power of a compelling Cause rests in the soul of its creator, because a Cause springs from the soul. It is a spiritual statement from *one* soul and cannot be the result of many. It comes from a deep place of knowing, some conviction that a richly imagined future could in some way, dramatically and positively, change the world. Others can offer their input, help, give advice, and even help to fine-tune, strengthen, and wordsmith it. But in the end, a magnetic Cause is a one-of-a-kind thing and cannot be cobbled together by a committee or a team. The myth that it can is pure hokum, and has resulted in the production of some of the world's most awful vision statements.

Leaders have dreams, passions, Causes. They want to change or improve the world and help people to realize *their* dreams because they know that the best way to predict the future is to create it. This Cause is a divine mission drawn from deep within their hearts. Sometimes, when first articulated, it may appear to be frail, because although the conceiver may see the magic clearly, they may find it harder to find the words that give voice to the future they imagine. A unique and great Cause describes a world that does not yet exist, and it is difficult to describe tomorrow in today's language. Often, for this reason, the natural human reaction is to resist the change offered by the Cause.

It is not because things are difficult that we do not dare, it is because we do not dare that they are difficult.

SENECA

Lack of literary elegance need not necessarily diminish a great Cause because great Causes have their own energy. What a great Cause may lack in precision and polish will be made up by its passion, beauty, and magnetism. While both are better, it is the latter that attracts parceners to the Cause.

7

Step Three

Enabling Parceners to Find Their Calling

After achieving pure clarity about their Destiny, then defining and championing the Cause, Inspirational Leaders **first reaffirm their commitment to their own Calling and then coach others to find and master theirs**. A Calling is a sense of authenticity and knowingness about one's gifts and talents, and an awareness of their relevance and applicability to a Cause. This vocational mastery and bliss must be experienced before it can be taught.

This chapter describes how leaders can best coach parceners to find their Calling. By default, I have made a rash assumption: that the leader has identified his or her own Calling. I have worked with and studied thousands of leaders around the world, and as a result, I have learned how few are really clear about their Calling. By the way, I believe more than half of all leaders that I have worked with would change their vocation to an avocation if they were presented with an opportunity to do so. This presents a conundrum: leaders cannot coach parceners to identify their genuine Calling if they do not know how to do so themselves. So, if there is any doubt whether you are practicing your true Calling today, please read this chapter as if it were speaking directly to you. If there is no doubt in your mind that your current path is indeed your true Calling, then please read this chapter as a guide to reconfirm your own Calling and then assist parceners in finding theirs.

How We Become Lost

Many of us are incapable of living our dreams at work and are frustrated in our attempts to achieve clarity around our vocation. We have come to believe that we can't live a full life while making a living. We fantasize and therefore blur the boundaries between fact and fiction, thus becoming immobilized between the two. As a result, we fail to put energy into our search for our real Calling. In *The Secret Life of Walter Mitty,* a classic 1947 movie loosely based on a James Thurber story, Danny Kaye plays the role of a magazine proof-reader, who merges the pulp fiction fantasies he reads for a living into his real life. Concocting elaborate delusions, he variously passes himself off as a Western outlaw, a swashbuckling sea captain, and a World War II fighter pilot. Eventually, no one is sure which is the mask and which is the real Walter Mitty — least of all, Walter Mitty. Some of us slide into a Mitty-esque entrainment in our lives, becoming so inauthentic that we eventually cannot tell the difference between the real and the surreal.

> **Most people sell their souls and live with a good conscience on the proceeds.**
> LOGAN P. SMITH

Few people ever discover the work they love, their Calling. Instead, we acquire skills based on an *I-must-earn-some-money* logic and then become slaves to them. We remain asleep in the dream of ego. We answer the question, "What do I want to do?" instead of, "How do I want to be in the Universe?" This causes us to be trapped in work that is not our Calling, that we do not love, and that does not inspire our heart. We become slaves to the illusion that the needs of the soul can be deferred while we feed our egos, and that the soul can operate independently of the ego. We fool ourselves with the myth that if we can get just one more promotion, one more mortgage payment, and one more child through college — then we will pursue our spiritual quests. But "just one more" always leads to "just one more." Like the horizon, it never comes closer, even though we advance towards it. As a result, our soul retreats from our work, and we feel empty. But doing work we love, that summons the soul, cannot be achieved by pursuing our skills alone. Our hearts and souls will only be fully engaged when we discover our natural gifts and then put them to great service in our lives. Our Calling is the work we love, the activities that we undertake that make our hearts soar and provide deep and lasting moments of bliss.

> **One's real life is often the life that one does not lead.**
> OSCAR WILDE

> **Life is a mystery to be lived, not a problem to be solved.**
> W.B. YEATS

Often, we confuse a Calling with a career or job. It is neither. Our Calling is the spiritual union of our passion with our essential, inherent talents,

Use what talent you possess: the woods would be very silent if no birds sang except those that sang best.

HENRY VAN DYKE

resulting in a holistic alignment of spirit with function. A job or a career limits us and encourages our smallness; the grandness of a Calling invites us to grow. A Calling is not a product of the ego or the personality; it is an extension of our soul. A Calling is just that — something we are being "called" to, by our muse, by an inner voice, by a higher presence, by something greater than us. A Calling draws us from our inner world to the outer world and integrates the two. Careers often lack integrity and authenticity; a Calling demands and invokes both. A Calling moves us from our dreams to actions. We honor our soul by responding positively to our Calling.

Reflect for a moment. What are the gifts with which you have been blessed, but which have been hidden from you or set aside because of your fear of failure? Are you engaged in work you value or work that merely pays the bills? Is your work spiritually *and* materially rewarding? Is your work your Calling? Do you love your work? What do you *love* to do? What are your *authentic*, natural gifts? When are you most happy in your life? What are you doing when that happens? How can you turn those activities into your life-work? How can you make your work your spiritual practice? What is holding you back? How can you overcome those obstacles? Millions of people today are asking profound questions about their work. Dramatic shifts in the balance and style of our lives can pivot on the answers to questions like these — and our reaction to them. We cannot become inspired, and, therefore, we cannot inspire others, until our gifts and our vocation are aligned, until we are practicing our Calling.

Finding joy in our work depends on the relationship between our soul and

We think too much. We feel too little.

CHARLIE CHAPLIN

our work, on the degree to which our work engages and nourishes our souls. Before embarking on a search for the work you love, test the relationship between your current work and your soul. Your answers will provide insight into the level of soulfulness in your work — whether you have found your Calling:

Is My Calling Aligned with My Soul? A Check-Up

The following questionnaire uses two words that are familiar to us everywhere in our lives, but often not at work: love and soul. Many old story leaders recoil when they hear these words, fearing that crystals and incense will follow. The dictionary defines love as a deep and tender feeling of affection.

IS MY CALLING ALIGNED WITH MY SOUL?

Please place a tick beside each question where you are able to answer YES.

1. I look forward to going to work on Monday mornings.	
2. At my organization we believe in and practice noble values.	
3. At work we tell the truth to employees, customers and suppliers.	
4. At work my colleagues keep the promises we make to employees, customers and suppliers.	
5. We have happy relationships with all employees, customers and suppliers.	
6. The leaders where I work do not use fear as a motivator.	
7. I love the people with whom I work.	
8. I have fun at work.	
9. I love the work I do.	
10. My work has meaning and richly rewards my Soul.	
11. My physical working environment is inspiring.	
12. My organization doesn't try to win by beating our competition.	
13. The products and services we sell are friendly to people and the planet.	
14. I have all the information and authority I need to do my job.	
15. I trust everyone with whom I work.	
16. My organization is not bureaucratic.	
17. I am encouraged to use all my creative potential at work.	
18. I am truly inspired by my work and colleagues.	
19. My work is valuable to my community.	
20. Every dollar earned by our organization makes my Soul proud.	

TOTAL

How to Score

Total the number of "Yeses" in the right-hand column and check your score against the numbers below to determine the interpretation that is appropriate for you.

- 0–4: Your Soul is endangered by your current work which is harmful to your spiritual well-being.
- 5–8: Your work is beginning to stir your Soul — nourish this. By doing so, you will regenerate yourself.
- 9–12: Your organization makes a valuable contribution to your Soul. There is much to do but you are on your way. The prospects for a fusion between your Soul and your work, between Calling and Cause, are excellent.
- 13–16: Congratulations! Your workplace is becoming a Sanctuary — a community of kindred Souls, in which your Soul can flourish and soar.
- 17–20: In your organization, work is a spiritual practice — cherish it! Your are in that sacred space where destiny, calling and cause are aligned.

(Adapted from *Reclaiming Higher Ground*, The Secretan Center, Alton, 2003)

Most people yearn for the opportunity to have deep and tender feelings of affection for their work and their colleagues. They want to do work they love, with people they care about. These are natural human aspirations that are strangely absent in the modern workplace. And then there is the "S" word — the Soul. The very notion of the soul, let alone the thought of having soulful experiences at work, mystifies many people. We all experience soulful moments in our lives — when we are at the symphony, when we watch a sunset, when we gaze into the eyes of our lover, when we hold a baby, when we play with a puppy, when we are deeply appreciated. We all want to feel the same way at work. There is no reason why this should not be so.

Hardly anybody fails at something that engages their hearts; they fail at things that are driven by negative energy. Fear, especially of poverty, inadequacy, loss of status, change, and other frailties of the ego, drive our career choices, and paradoxically, this inevitably leads us to failure — the thing we fear most. What makes great artists, poets, athletes, or writers unique is that they are among the few who have discovered their gifts and turned them into work that they love. It is a Calling, a vocation. As a consequence, they are often brilliant in their fields.

Being in the Moment, Not on a Journey

THE KINGDOM OF HEAVEN

We do not have to die to enter the Kingdom of Heaven. In fact, we have to be fully alive. When we breathe in and out and hug a beautiful tree, we are in Heaven. When we take one conscious breath, aware of our eyes, our heart, our liver, and our non-toothache, we are transported to Paradise right away. Peace is available. We only have to touch it. When we are truly alive, we can see that the tree is part Heaven, and we are also part of Heaven. The whole universe is conspiring to reveal this to us, but we are so out of touch that we invest our resources in cutting down the trees. If we want to enter Heaven on Earth, we need only one conscious step and one conscious breath. When we touch peace, everything becomes real. We become ourselves, fully alive in the present moment, and the tree, our child, and everything else reveal themselves to us in their full splendor. The miracle is not to walk on thin air or water, but walk on Earth.

THICH NHAT HAHN, *TOUCHING PEACE*[25]

We often hear that life is a journey, but perhaps it is not so much a journey as a collection of moments. We are not destined to achieve a certain standard of living or a particular set of career goals — such ambitions are typically modern, narcissistic notions that have become the hallmark of the baby-boom generation. Real living is not about tolerating the moments of work along the journey to retirement in order to build a fat retirement fund.

Your work is to discover your work, and then with all your heart to give yourself to it.
BUDDHA

The point of life is not to slave away to the age of sixty-five and then say, "Phew! Glad that's over!" We are destined to live each moment joyfully, passionately, and in the service of others. This is a definition of bliss, and bliss is an essential requirement of the soul — whether at work *or* at play.

Nothing should be prized more highly than the value of each day.
GOETHE

Finding the work that you love is not complicated or difficult; it just requires *clarity, choice, and commitment.* We need to curb our addiction to personality (or ego) gratification and open our hearts to options that nourish the soul. Think about your health. There are no mysteries to becoming fitter, nor is it complicated or difficult. It simply requires clarity, choice, and commitment:

- *Clarity:* knowing that one must change and establishing a goal, for example, losing weight
- *Choice:* changing diet perhaps, exercising and working out, restoring greater balance in one's life, and
- *Commitment:* following the regimen

When we are not prepared to make these choices and commitments, we are unlikely to progress towards our aspirations, even if they are clear, and when we cling to the status quo, we are saying to ourselves, "I do not have the courage to change."

The highest reward for a person's toil is not what they get for it, but what they become of it.
JOHN RUSKIN

It is the same with our work. Identifying work that would inspire our soul is not a difficult process. The difficult part is having the courage to make the appropriate choices and committing to them. If you are a high-powered executive or leader enjoying all the creature comforts that material success can buy, but hating every moment of your work, the choice is simple:

change your work from the inside out so that you can be happy in it, or quit and find the work you love. The question is, "Do you have the courage to give up the security, toys and perceived esteem that being a material success but spiritual derelict provides?" Millions of people, nearly half the working population according to our research, cannot bring themselves to make the sacrifices needed. They stay in a rut and complain for the rest of their lives that they never found the work they loved. This is the old story: no pain, no gain. Of course, the real pain comes from being imprisoned in work that does not inspire the soul. On the other hand, finding work that is our spiritual practice is achieved when we make the personal commitment to reduce dependency on the things that feed the personality and instead find and develop pursuits that nourish the soul.

Follow Your Intuition

Scott Adams toiled in his cubicle at Pacific Bell for years before being "downsized" by the firm in 1995. This personal inconvenience proved to be just the catalyst he had been waiting for to release his pals Dilbert, Catbert, Dogbert, Ratbert, and the Boss into an unsuspecting but eager world. Today, Scott Adams is one of the world's most successful cartoonists, having found his Calling by speaking to the hearts of millions of cubicle-dwellers around the globe.

In 1994, Jeff Bezos gave up his cushy job as a vice-president on Wall Street and headed for the West Coast with the idea of selling books over the Internet. Five days later, he had set up his new company in his basement. Today, Amazon.com is the most successful company on the Web and the largest bookseller in the world. Bezos had found his Calling: redefining how to sell to the masses in an electronic marketplace.

For some, their Calling becomes very clear early in their lives. Steven Spielberg won his first film award for a forty-minute fully scripted action movie when he was thirteen. Fred Smith, founder and chairman of Federal Express, conceived the idea for an overnight delivery service while an undergraduate at Yale University. Leo Burnett borrowed against his life insurance policy and mortgaged his home to come up with the money to establish one of the greatest advertising agencies in the world. In 1922, twenty-one-year-old George Gallup took a job at the *St. Louis Post-Dispatch* surveying city readers to determine their interests, and the eponymous Gallup Poll entered in to our lexicon. Lillian Vernon was a young pregnant housewife when she launched her catalog from her kitchen table, eventually forming the Lillian Vernon Corporation, which received over 5 million orders by mail in 1999. Virgin Group Inc. Chairman and CEO, Richard Branson, ran his first advertisement for Virgin Records in the final issue of his magazine *Student* when he was — a student.

Music is Love in search of a word.

SIDNEY LANIER

Some of us don't have an inner voice shouting clear directions, so we respond to the urgings of parents who guide us into business, law, dentistry, medicine, a craft, trade, or profession, believing it to be "the best thing" for us. We cruise along the highway of life in this way until we realize there is more. The subtle urging from our soul yearns to be heard. We long to follow our dreams, to paint in technicolor instead of monochrome. We long for meaning and fulfillment, to honor our souls. We dream about flying at last.

For many, though, set in their ways for so long, they think it is too late. They seem incapable of thinking out of the box, perhaps even burning the box, because it seems so outrageous at this

To be nobody but yourself in a world which is doing its best to make you everybody else — means to fight the hardest battle which any human being can fight and never stop fighting.

e.e. cummings

stage of their lives. There is an old story about the middle-aged woman who yearned to play the piano. After deciding to follow her life-long dream, she announced to a friend that she had changed her mind and was abandon- ing her plans. When her friend asked why, she explained that it would take ten years to learn how to master the piano, and that since she was fifty, this meant that she would be sixty before she achieved her goal. Her friend thought for a moment before observing, "But darling, what difference will it make — you will be sixty anyway!" Too often we invent roadblocks and convince ourselves that our dreams are beyond our reach. We rationalize our resistance to change.

If there is any point at all to life, surely it is to live out our dreams, to serve, to follow our bliss, to release the music within us, play it with joy, and to share it with others? Surely we have a responsibility to finally listen to, and honor, the siren calls of our souls that have been silenced by our egos throughout our lives? How else can we connect with our essence, the source of our Calling?

There Is No Calling without Caring and Service

Caring, or serving others, is a necessary condition of happiness both in work and in life generally. A Calling without a significant component of service is not a Calling. When we serve others, we transform work into a Calling.

Everyone can be great because everyone can serve.

MARTIN LUTHER KING, JR.

Inspirational Leader Jim Paquette joined the Sisters of Charity of Leavenworth Health Services Corporation nineteen years ago to serve, first as CFO of a hospital, then as CEO of the same unit and more recently as CEO for the Montana Region. His Destiny is "to do Christ's work on Earth." Jim says, "I am fortunate to work for an organization where I can state this openly. Our Mission calls for us to 'join ourselves to the healing ministry of Jesus, to offer the best and most compassionate care within our power to the people of Montana and surrounding regions, with special concern for those who lack such care and for those who are poor.' " How does this compare to the mission statement in your organization? Does your mission statement have the power to lift your spirit in the way these words do for Jim? Does it align tightly with your Destiny and your Calling and inspire you in the same way that Jim is inspired, so that he, in turn, inspires others?

I never knew how to worship until I knew how to love.

HENRY WARD BEECHER

Jim tells the story of the difficult times he was having setting up a heart unit at St. Vincent's Hospital and also dealing with the crash of a helicopter in which the pilot and patient were both killed. As he was leaving to go home one Friday evening, his phone rang. It was his director, the president of the Health Service Corporation, Sister Macrina Ryan from Kansas. She asked how Jim was doing and inquired about his family. Then she asked how things were going at the hospital. Jim walked her through the financial trials and challenges he was facing. Sister Macrina said she was aware of all the issues. Then she continued, "I want you to know that we are praying for you and keeping you in our thoughts." Sister Macrina wasn't asking about the metrics. She had heard about the other issues and was asking how Jim was *feeling*. Jim Paquette reflected recently on this experience: "I was pretty confident that the President of GE rarely, if ever, got a call like that from the Chair of his or her Board. This is a caring organization and that caring starts at the very top."

Jim is well known in the healthcare industry as an outstanding Inspirational Leader who inspires and serves others. The golden thread that runs from his Destiny, to his Calling, to his desire to serve is solid and true. That's why Jim's parceners love him.

Wynton Marsalis, the world-renowned jazz trumpet player, spends much of his life touring, recording, and winning Grammy awards. But he also uses his talents to serve — teaching underprivileged kids — in over one thousand schools during the last decade alone. Marsalis knows he is a great musician, but he also knows that one of his greatest gifts is to listen to the soul of a musician. He says, "When they play and I hear their sound, I can tell what kind of grades they make in school and what kind of habits they have. I can just hear it in their sound. I know what they're saying. Sometimes what they're saying is 'Help.' "[26] The opportunity to serve by sharing our gifts is the highest Calling, and we are gifted with the highest rewards in return: our hearts are infused with moments of pure bliss.

It is popularly believed that women live longer than men do. On the face of it, this is true. The average male lifespan in the United States is seventy-three and the average for women is seventy-nine. But gender does not tell us the whole story. John Allman and his colleagues at the California Institute of Technology have shown that longevity is more determined by which parent is the caregiver of their offspring and the amount of effort put into it. To support their contention that the caregiving sex (female usually) lives longer and healthier lives, Allman investigated ten primates, including man. Because female chimpanzees are very promiscuous, most male chimpanzees have no idea who their children are. Consequently, male chimpanzees take virtually no interest in any children. Female chimpanzees live on average about 40% longer than their male companions. On the other hand, many gorillas make longer-term bonds with their female partners, and therefore form closer relationships with offspring that they know are their own. Male gorillas are much closer to their offspring, although far less so than females and, as a consequence, female gorillas live 12.5% longer than males. For the same reasons, women live 8% longer than men.

One might conclude that the longevity of females and their greater role as caregivers for their children is coincidental. Since 99% of all mammals are raised by the female species, this conclusion might be justified — barring the exceptions revealed by analysis of the 1% of mammals where males raise their offspring. The Titi monkey and the Owl monkey are both examples of fathers who carry their children around until they are able to move safely and independently through the trees. Offspring of both cling tenaciously to the fur of their father and are only briefly transferred to their mothers during nursing periods. If the father dies, the mother will abandon the babies, who will usually die, too. In the case of the Titi and Owl monkeys, males live 20% longer than females. Natural selection, and evolution, is not as merciless as we think — nature rewards care-giving parents with longevity. Nature rewards those who serve.

Identifying Your Calling

Our Calling is a siren that sings to our heart throughout our lives. Sometimes it sings softly, sometimes our egos suppress it, sometimes is sings like Callas or Pavarotti. Whatever the intensity, whatever the style, our Calling strains to be heard, sending us signals throughout our lives in an endless stream of creative efforts to make itself noticed. Our purpose is to listen attentively, to use every means we can to turn up the volume of the siren within, so that we can clearly hear the song of our Calling. The striking thing about a Calling is that it never goes away. If we cannot realize our Calling, we will die with our music still within us.

> **I slept and dreamt that life was Joy, and then I awoke and realized that life was Duty, And then I went to work — and, lo and behold I discovered that Duty can be Joy.**
>
> RABINDRANATH TAGORE

James Hillman has written, "The soul in each of us is given a unique daemon before we are born, and it has selected an image or pattern that we live on earth. This soul–companion, the daemon, guides us here; in the process of arrival, however, we forget all that took place and believe we come empty into this world. The daemon remembers what is in your image and belongs to your pattern, and therefore your daemon is the carrier of your destiny." [27]

The Pre-Probability Plane

For each of us, there is one true Calling. It is our potential, waiting to manifest. It is not something we become *trained* for — it is something we are *called* to. We do not bend ourselves to fit something, but we embrace that which invites us. Contrary to what we are taught to believe, and contrary to the theories of psychologists, we are not the result of our social conditioning or our genetic heritage. We are capable of identifying our Calling through the use of insightful tools and releasing our intentionality into the Universal Energy Field, where there resides the conditions, opportunities, networks, skills, training, knowledge, and wisdom necessary for us to follow our Calling.

The underlying source of all life is the *quantum void*, the reality from which all life emerges. At the subatomic level, the Universe consists of raw energy, and in this quantum void, this raw energy isn't anything — it just *is*. The quantum void is not empty — it is full of everything that ultimately manifests itself on the surface of life — what our senses detect. The quantum void represents potential and probability, with the *capability* of manifesting into consciousness. It is from here that we are able to change probabilities into realities. When we do this, we are converting the invisible into the visible. These probabilities reside within what I call the *Pre-Probability Plane*.

Whether or not these probabilities are manifested into the conscious energy field, the universal awareness of all living things, depends on our intentions — what we call *intentionality*. Intentionality is energy from the conscious energy field calling on the *Pre-Probability Plane* for the information necessary to trigger probabilities. A plant must call upon the unrealized energy of the sun in order to sustain itself and grow. It must also monitor the entire celestial domain in order to ensure that it is perfectly receptive to nutrients and light, rests when necessary in order to conserve energy, grow, and replicate. It also draws data and energy from the *Pre-Probability Plane* in order to build cells, create roots, and establish systems of osmosis, nutrition, and photosynthesis. An acorn without intentionality will remain an acorn. An acorn *with* intentionality will reach into the *Pre-Probability Plane* and draw the information necessary to become a mighty oak tree.

Examples of intentionality bringing about the desired manifested outcome

A human being is part of a whole called, by us, universe. A part limited in time and space, he experiences himself, his thoughts and feelings as something separated from the rest. A kind of optical delusion of his consciousness. This delusion is a kind of prison for us restricting us to our personal desires and to affection for a few persons nearest to us. Our task must be to free ourselves from this prison by widening our circle of compassion, to embrace all living creatures and the whole nature in its beauty.

ALBERT EINSTEIN

are evident everyday in our lives. A placebo is intentionality disguised as a pill. Prayer is intentionality in the form of an invocation. Miracles are the results of collective intentionality. Complementary medical practices such as acupuncture and homeopathy are techniques of intentionality designed to activate the knowledge desired from the *Pre-Probability Plane.*

Intentionality is thought, and thought is energy. Energy operates at various frequencies, and consequently humans (who are a manifestation of energy) function at different frequencies. The most commonly experienced frequency is our body — our physiological energy frequency. Indeed, for many people, this is the only frequency with which they are familiar. Our personal growth and spiritual evolution access different, higher frequencies — spiritual energy frequencies. When we meditate, we are functioning at yet another, higher frequency. When our meditation reaches the level of trance, where our physiological activity slows or stops, but our experience continues, we have reached yet another, higher level of frequency. When we experience our sense of being one with the Universe, we are operating at another, higher level frequency; and when we sense our experience of being one with God, we operate at the highest frequency. When we function at the highest of these frequencies, we are close to the *Pre-Probability Plane.* It is here that we are closest to the field of unrealized probabilities, the state of raw energy and potential. This is the subquantum level, the quantum void, before the conscious energy field is activated by intentionality. This is where we access our soul.

All Souls are one with the Oversoul.

THE SECRET DOCTRINE,
ALICE A. BAILEY

Synchronicity: The Result of Intentionality

Traditionally, we are encouraged to survey the marketplace in order to identify the strengths and range of opportunities, occupations, and the careers that offer the greatest potential rewards and meet our future needs. After gathering this information, we embark on paths designed to secure our ideal career — dentistry, law, medicine, teaching, business, crafts or the arts, for example. Some of us have no plan, accidentally falling into a life lived as a victim or as a result. In these circumstances, we are the product of our heredity, our genes, and the external environment — and the absence of intentionality.

What all this presents is a picture of humanity as prisoners of limited possibility thinking. It is a uni-dimensional view that does not go beyond our own ego and personality or the personalities of others; it fails to consider the spiritual potential within each of us and within the Universe.

You are searching for the magic key that will unlock the door to the source of power; and yet you have the key in your own hands.

NAPOLEON HILL

As James Hillman points out, "By accepting the idea that I am the effect of a subtle buffeting between hereditary and societal forces, I reduce myself to a result. The more my life is accounted for by what already occurred in my chromosomes, by what my parents did or didn't do and by my early years now long past, the more my biography is the story of a victim."[28]

By listening to the siren within, however, and by following paths fueled by our passion and inner knowing, our values and the energy of our intentionality, and then using this to access the energy resting in the form of potential in the *Pre-Probability Plane*, we can manifest any Calling that our heart and soul desires.

Yet our lack of faith in the Divine, our sense of frailty, unworthiness, and insecurity cause us to invent words like *synchronicity*. Synchronicity is the arrival of a timely reality called forth by intentionality from the preprobability plane. Synchronicity is proof that we can manifest realities that on the face of it seem outrageous — even miraculous.

Synchronicity is normal behavior. Look at the formations of nature, the flight paths of birds and insects, the directions and shapes and sizes in which grass grows, the shapes, strengths, direction, height, content and impact of clouds, the physical, emotional, and energetic diversity of humans.

You are never given a wish without also being given the power to make it true.

RICHARD BACH

Synchronicity is the rule, not the exception of nature. Synchronicity is where the factors of intentionality converge. Though synchronicity may seem random to the untrained eye, to the mystic, to the Aquarian leader, it is nothing less than the manifestation of intended outcomes.

Intentionality

I live and work in the countryside. Animals of all kinds visit us from nature and many plants choose to live around us, beyond the ones that we have planted. A few years ago, I had the driveway to our offices paved to better withstand the growing traffic. The intentionality of the lilies of the valley, now paved over, remained as strong as ever — my ego (the asphalt) was not strong enough to stop the intentionality of the lilies of the valley from thrusting through the asphalt. The lilies had registered their intentionality and called for the information necessary from the *Pre-Probability Plane* and consequently manifested the reality they desired. Relatively speaking, this is a very large obstacle which, scaled up to the human level, would probably thwart most of us. What determines outcomes is the relative level of power of the intention.

> **Miracles happen, not in opposition to nature, but in opposition to what we know of nature.**
>
> ST. AUGUSTINE

How do we build this level of power? Paradoxically, we do it in the opposite way one would have assumed: *we let go.*

In March of 1998, Gilbert Ortiz learned from his doctor that he had failing kidneys and an inch-long aneurysm on his aorta. "I was feeling bad," the seventy-year-old Ortiz said. "I was done, really done." On the very same day, Ortiz's wife Emma went to their Cheyenne, Wyoming, mailbox. There were two letters. One dated November 28, 1981, was from Mother Teresa, and the other was from the superior of the Missionaries of Charity, Sister Nirmala Joshi. The superior's letter reminded Gilbert Ortiz that he had written Mother Teresa seventeen years earlier and had never received a reply. After Mother Teresa had died in September of 1997, her original response to Ortiz's letter had been found at the Order's house in New York in February, 1998.

"Although the content of the letter may not be important or relevant now, nearly seventeen years later," Joshi wrote, "we thought you might like to have the letter since it bears Mother's signature."

In her letter to Ortiz, Mother Teresa wrote, "Pain, sorrow, suffering, is but the kiss of Jesus. A sign that you have come so close to him that he can kiss you. May God give you all the courage to accept your cross with resignation and love in union with the passion of Jesus. God Bless you."

Ortiz had released intentionality into the pre-potential plane seventeen years earlier and was eventually rewarded. "When I read that letter, I hit the roof. Maybe I hit heaven," Ortiz said. "If Christ wants to take me, I'm ready to go. Now I know I've got somebody praying for me. Now when I get to heaven, I've got somebody I have to meet, and it's Mother Teresa."

A Course in Miracles says, "There is no order of difficulty in miracles." We often think that miracles only happen in mythology, to contemporary saints, gurus, and bodhisattva. But mere mortals like you and I can open

> How lovely to think that no one need wait a moment: we can start now, start slowly changing the world! How lovely that everyone, great and small, can make a contribution towards introducing justice straightaway.
>
> ANNE FRANK

ourselves to the possibility of miracles every day. We must become comfortable trusting the Universe, to learn to appreciate the extraordinary as ordinary. Let me give you an example.

I was privileged to spend nearly a week with Deepak Chopra in La Jolla, California. Though I had been practicing meditation for thirty-five years, first transcendental meditation and later various forms of Zazen and breathing meditation, I took the opportunity to learn an entirely different form — Primordial Sound Meditation. When I returned home, I turned my attention to an upcoming project, the certification of thirty-five new Associates of the Secretan Center. I wanted to teach them while they were in a meditative state. I put this intention out to the universal field and released it. I did not think of it again for several weeks. As I was preparing the curriculum for the Secretan Center Certification Program, it occurred to me

> Nature does nothing uselessly.
>
> ARISTOTLE

that we could teach all of them Primordial Sound Meditation. I searched the Internet for a teacher and found one in Toronto, an hour's drive from where I live in Canada. I called her to see if she would be interested in teaching meditation. Her name was Helen Goldstein, and when she answered the telephone, she said, "I have been praying for a call like this. Apart from teaching meditation, I run the largest yoga school in Canada. But my calling is to change the world by working with the business community, and until now I have not found the path. I was praying for a call; I knew I would get one and, although I know your work, I didn't know it would be you." Our lives became entwined in each other's Causes as a result of what some would call synchronicity, others a miracle. But if you are used to assembling your desired reality from the *Pre-Probability Plane*, through intentionality, you will look upon it as simply a magical, divine, but everyday, occurrence.

Helen had a government contract on the dates I asked her to teach our Associates, but her government client moved the dates. Helen taught Primordial Sound Meditation to all of our Associates, and this enabled us to teach part of our curriculum to Associates while they were in a meditative state. Helen fulfilled one of her dreams by becoming an Associate, thus learning to combine her gifts with our expertise, thereby fulfilling her ambition to work much more closely with corporate executives.

Perhaps the only limits to what can be manifested from the *Pre-Probability Plane* are those imposed by our minds.

The Case of Bernie Krause

Bernie Krause began studying classical music at the age of three in his native Detroit. He graduated to composition at age four and then to guitar as an adolescent. After college, he worked in radio and concert promotion and as a studio musician for the *Soupy Sales Show*. After a year as a member of the Weavers folk-singing group, he became a producer and studio musician for Motown records before moving to Los Angeles. With his then business partner Paul Beaver, Krause invested in one of the first Moog synthesizers, eventually contributing to over 250 albums, including ones by The Byrds, The Doors, Mick Jagger, and George Harrison.

When love and skill work together, expect a masterpiece.

JOHN RUSKIN

Though Krause had not yet found his true Calling, he relied heavily on the most important asset of those searching for their Calling: intentionality. Krause worked on a project called *Wild Sanctuary*, the first album to use sounds collected from the natural environment. The experience of tape-recording the sounds of the California surf and blending them into lush orchestral instrumentation led to an epiphany for Krause. "From then on," he says, "every spare moment, I was outside with a microphone."

Being alert to our inner voice during the search is critical to discovering the right livelihood. Krause pushed the envelope, searching for ever more exotic sounds. When scientists would not let him accompany them because they felt he was unqualified for scientific expeditions, he countered their skepticism by studying successfully for his Ph.D. in bioacoustics. This enabled him to travel to the Alaskan tundra, to famed primate expert Jane Goodall's camp in Tanzania, to Borneo, Indonesia, Sumatra, to rainforests, mountains, oceans, deserts, and the Amazon. He recorded ants, frogs, insect larva, sperm whales, earthworms, gibbons, and snails. He recorded the sounds of a water-parched cottonwood tree drinking noisily after an intense rainfall. He has amassed 3,500 hours of habitat sounds during his thirty-year career, recording the voices of fifteen thousand creatures. During that time, 20% of the habitats have become extinct, and Krause sees his work as a mission — he donates a percentage of his profits to organi-

**May you live
all the days of
your life.**

JONATHAN

SWIFT

zations such as the Nature Conservancy. His CDs have sold over 1.5 million copies, and he has contributed to over 130 feature films, including *Apocalypse Now* and *Rosemary's Baby*. He has been assaulted by a cobra, hurled by a gorilla, and put upon by a polar bear, but he found his Calling, and every day of that Calling is an earthly day in heaven for Bernie Krause.[29]

Letting Go

Outlined below is a meditation to help you to prepare yourself for the practice of letting go. Please read the following sentences slowly, pausing after each one, inviting their meaning to trickle gently into your consciousness. After each sentence, reflect and then breathe deeply and pause before proceeding to the next one...

- Acknowledge your desire to be an instrument of the Universe.

- Give thanks for life as it is.

- Let go of your anger, sadness, and fears.

- Move your heart and mind out of your current space/time awareness.

- Adopt an attitude of surrender; go with the flow.

- Think like a mystic, in Thomas Merton's definition of this term: adopt a complete, unqualified sense of wonder about life.

Close your eyes and practice the thoughts above; repeat them in the same sequence for a few more moments...then continue to read the following sentences slowly, pausing after you read each one to let them trickle into your consciousness...

It is from a mystical perspective that we are enabled to manifest what we need from the *Pre-Probability Plane*. It is from this framework that we ready ourselves to call in the information from the *Pre-Probability Plane*, which we do in the following way:

- Gather your intent and release it into the Universe.

- Keep your ego out of the equation. No matter how difficult this may seem at times, it is an essential prerequisite.

Close your eyes and practice the thoughts above, repeat them in the same sequence, for a moment or two...

- Practice the Buddhist concept of detachment from the outcome.

A Meditation: Finding Your Calling

Meditation is the uninterrupted flow of energy on the subject being meditated on. One of the elements of meditation is stillness, which is a part of all great religions and wisdom teachings. One of the purposes of meditation is a paradox: to find things by letting go of them. When you know you don't know, then you don't know you know.

Performance metrics and measures are an ever present fact of business life. The old adage "What gets done gets measured" stands guard over our work lives. Many people believe that if you do not analyze the results of our work with some form of numeric calipers, it is not real or experienced. Dr. J. Evans Pritchard, the poetry analyst in *Dead Poet's Society*, was an example. We are counseled to create plans for achieving our goals by using these data. Though many may not believe this, there are other ways to measure the realities and experiences of life, and other ways to achieve our dreams. Indeed, there are many aspects of our lives which will simply not yield to conventional metrics. How do you measure the way a beautiful sunset touches your soul? What stirs inside you when you hear beautiful music or poetry? Or the inner sensations when walking in your bare feet along the soft sand at the ocean's edge? What criteria would you use to measure the visceral experience of holding a newborn baby? What is the financial or quantitative measurement of being "in flow" or being transported to a different plane when lost in the practice of doing something you love? How does one plot a chart or graph of being deeply in love? Is there a ten-point scale for measuring a profound sense of gratitude? How do you define the moment when you feel at one with the Universe? Or when you are passionately engaged in your faith? These are moments that touch your soul and are as real, perhaps more so, than many other so-called measurable experiences in life.

Meditation is one of the most powerful ways to access information in our lives. It is a means of calming our minds, reducing the mental chatter in our heads, and opening up our subconscious to information that we do not normally see, hear or sense in any other way. Without meditation, we tend to be blocked, to miss the obvious and to be closed to information and energy that is striving to connect us to our Destiny. Meditation is a powerful way to open the heart and the soul, as well as the mind to the boundless possibilities that might be ours if we pay attention. After all, we are nothing more than potential; we are spiritual and human beings seeking a relationship with our appropriate future.

We need to listen, to follow our inner voice and pay heed to the spiritual call, what Carl Jung called *the unavoidable vocation towards individuation*. In this way, we may live our passion, deliver our best work, and make our best contribution. The meditation below invites you to open your inner ear so that you can hear the siren within singing to your heart, inviting you to recognize your Calling. If you want to listen to this meditation, please go to the Secretan Center website at <http://www.secretan.com>.

A Meditation: Finding Your Calling

(**Note:** Find a friend to be your guide for this meditation. This should be someone close to you whom you trust and who will support you in every way in this quest for your Calling. Ask them to read the following meditation very slowly, modulating their voice, articulating and enunciating deliberately and slowly. Please do not do the meditation unless you have at least two hours available. Once you have begun, do not rush any of the phases of the meditation and ask your guide to be aware of your transcendental state and safety at all times. If you know a meditation teacher or master, invite their support in guiding you through this meditation. Do not complete any part of this meditation if it could trigger any personal physical or mental weaknesses you might have or if it could pose any medical risk to you.)

First, find a comfortable place in which to sit. If you meditate regularly, then you will probably find a cross-legged position comfortable. If not, then sit on a chair with your feet flat on the ground, your back upright and pressed firmly against a solid support, thus permitting energy to freely flow directly up and down your spine. Place your hands on your knees with your palms upright, thus inviting the universal energy to flow through you.

If you wish to play music that soothes the soul, do so very softly. Make sure that you are not distracted by the music and that it will not be necessary to attend to it during your meditation.

If you wish, you may light a candle. Make sure that there are no distractions around you and that you will not be disturbed.

Close your eyes and sit quietly for a few moments and concentrate on your breathing — take some slow, deep breaths. Repeat this slow deep inhalation and exhalation as you settle into a gentle but deep breathing rhythm. Keep your attention focused on your breathing.

(Pause ... focus on your steady breathing)

This is a meditation of intentionality, so let's begin with the intention of healing your body, the temple for your soul.

Continue to concentrate on your breathing.

Think for a moment about those things that you are currently angry about.

(Pause ... focus on your steady breathing)

Now let them go. Gently release them from your mind. Continue to concentrate on your breathing.

Slowly repeat to yourself the phrase, "I invite the Divine presence of the Creator." (The Creator is the Higher Presence, as you understand it.) Repeat this again several times — "I invite the Divine presence of the Creator." Continue to repeat the phrase for four or five minutes.

(Pause ... focus on your steady breathing)

Very slowly, scan your body with your third eye. As you do so, silence your mental chatter. Focus your energy within your physical body. After a few moments, slowly scan from the top of your head to the tip of your toes. Pause as you observe in your mind, every part of your body. Along the way, gently relax every area of tension. Don't forget areas like your throat, your cheeks, your jaws and tongue, your chest and tummy, arms and hands, knees, calves, feet, and toes — including each knuckle and joint. Continue to concentrate on your deep breathing and repeating "I invite the Divine presence of the Creator."

Bring your awareness to your heart and become aware of its beat as it sends the life force throughout your body. As you concentrate on your heart, gently slow your heartbeat down.

(Pause ... focus on your steady breathing as it slows down with your heartbeat)

Bring your awareness to your blood flow within your body, and become aware of the friendly role your heart is playing in this process. Notice any areas in your body that are painful and concentrate on them for a moment, bringing heat to them. Become aware of the tingling and warmth in these sensitive areas as the blood flow and temperature increase.

Continue to breathe slowly and deeply in an even rhythm.

Continue to let go of any remaining anger.

While you are breathing deeply, your body is healing, and your mind is clearing itself of all other things. Bring your awareness to your passion — to what gives you the greatest joy in your life. Now define all of the mastery you could imagine you possess when you see this passion flourishing. Imagine your passion as a Calling and yourself practicing this Calling to the highest levels humanly attainable. Image your Calling being practiced by you to perfection.

Capture this picture in a ball of white light and hold it in your heart. Keep breathing steadily and deeply and repeating the phrase, "I invite the Divine intervention of the Creator."

While holding this image within the ball of white light in your heart, travel now to the Pre-Probability Plane, where all the information you need for your Calling rests as pure potential.

Prepare yourself to receive all of the guidance you need to find your Calling by saying softly and silently to yourself, "I am ready to receive." Repeat this phrase for four or five minutes. Keep your awareness on your breathing, which should be rhythmic, steady and deep.

Stay calmly in this place for a few moments.

Now, gently return from the Pre-Probability Plane by riding an arc of light back to the ball of white light in your heart, thus connecting the future to the present.

(Pause ... focus on your steady breathing)

It is now time to let go of your intentionality because you have now put it out into the Universe, into the Pre-Probability Plane. Your desires will manifest themselves in space/time reality — of this there is no doubt. It is only the timing that is uncertain. This is in the hands of the Universe. Repeat silently "I trust the Universe."

Prepare yourself to slowly return to an awakened state.

Concentrate on your breathing. When you are ready, slowly return to the present moment. Take your time, and when the moment is right, open your eyes.

Step Four

Aligning Calling and Cause

After achieving pure clarity about their Destiny, defining and championing the Cause, reaffirming their commitment to their own Calling, and coaching others to find and master theirs, **the Inpirational Leader aligns the two by enabling parceners to invest the energy of their Calling in service of the Cause**. When parceners hear about, and are drawn to, the Cause for the Inspirational Leader, the leader asks them, "What is your Calling?" and then proceeds to help them identify their true Calling and maximize their mastery within it. Thus, parceners make a passionate and seamless connection between their Calling and the Cause, achieving full alignment with the two.

All of us who work in organizations want to know five things about our work:

1. How does my work help to achieve the Cause?
2. Does my work enable me to use my deepest creative gifts?
3. Will my work make a difference to the world, will it have meaning, and will it make the world a better place?
4. How does my work meet my spiritual needs?
5. Is this how I want to be in the Universe?

Creating a Seamless Fit

These are the five issues which Inspirational Leaders discuss extensively with parceners, ensuring that satisfactory answers are found for each of them. Inspirational Leaders know that lifting the hearts of parceners is achieved through providing positive answers to these five issues more than the corporate measure of any bottom-line performance. This is not to say that the latter is not important, just that it leads us to the path of motivation, and we are more concerned with finding the path of inspiration. Inspirational Leaders work hard to help parceners align their work to the Cause, searching for a perfect, seamless fit between the work and the Calling of each parcener and the Cause.

A great Cause positions the connection we have with our work and the world on higher ground. It shifts our consciousness so profoundly, that we completely reframe our view of our work, so that it is no longer a boring functional statement, but a brilliant spiritual one that defines our connection with the Divine and the way we serve others. It moves work from the mundane to the inspiring. Bill Pollard says, "We have found that people want to work for a Cause, not just a living, and when there is an alignment between the [Cause] of the firm and the [Calling] of its people, a creative power is unleashed that results in quality service to the customer and the growth and development of the people serving. People find meaning in their work. The [Cause] becomes an organizing principle of effectiveness.

"Why is Shirley, a housekeeper in a 250-bed community hospital, still excited about her work after fifteen years? She certainly has seen some changes. She has moved from 2 West to 3 East and actually cleans more rooms today than she did five years ago. The chemicals, the mop, the housekeeping cart have all been improved. Nevertheless, the bathrooms and the toilets are still the same. The dirt has not changed, nor have the unexpected spills of the patients or the arrogance of some of the physicians. So what [inspires] Shirley? Does she have a mission in her work? Is her job just cleaning floors or is she part of a team of people that helps sick people get well? Is she recognized not only for what she does, but also for what she is becoming? Does she know that she is needed and is providing an important contribution?

"Shirley sees her job as extending to the welfare of the patient in the bed and as an integral part of a team supporting the work of the doctors and nurses — she has a Cause — a Cause that involves the health and welfare of others. When Shirley first came to us over fifteen years ago, no doubt she was merely looking for just a job. But she brought to her work an unlocked potential and a desire to accomplish something significant. As I talked with Shirley about her job, she shared with me her 'Cause' when she said: 'If we don't clean with a quality effort, we can't keep the doctors and nurses in business. We can't serve the patients. This place would be closed if we didn't have housekeeping.' Shirley was confirming the reality of our [Cause]."

The California Public Employees Retirement System (CalPERS) is committed to outstanding investment management in order to maximize the retirement benefits that will eventually be paid out to its members. Kayla G. Gillan, a thirty-eight-year-old mother of two daughters, joined CalPERS in 1986 after graduating from University of California Davis School of Law with a juris doctorate. She worked closely with founding guru, Dale M. Hanson, and former General Counsel Richard H. Koppes as Staff Counsel. In that position, "She's been in the wings for years, and has had to take all sorts of potshots," says Sarah A. Teslik, Director of the Council of Institutional Investors. But Gillan soon learned to contribute to and align with the Cause of CalPERS. Hanson and Koppes helped to align Gillan's prodigious legal talents to their Cause, by identifying weaknesses in the corporate governance of companies in which CalPERS held investments and deciding that their substantial stakes could be leveraged into improving the performance of these organizations. Their reasoning was that if corporate governance improved, corporate performance would improve, and so therefore would the values of CalPERS' investments held on behalf of members. As CalPERS Deputy Counsel from 1990–1996, Gillan aligned her research and legal skills with the Cause of CalPERS to convince companies like Apple, Fleming Cos., IBM, Sears, Roebuck & Co., Reebok, and Stride Rite Corp. to make changes that would lead to higher corporate performance. Since August 1996, Gillan has been CalPERS' General Counsel. She led a shareholder lawsuit against Walt Disney Co. claiming Michael D. Eisner and the Disney board acted irresponsibly when they paid at least $93 million in severance payments to former President Michael Ovitz, who left after just one year with Disney. CalPERS had a lot at stake — it owned 3.5 million Disney shares worth $271 million. Gillan was particularly concerned that when the deal was made with Ovitz, Eisner assured himself a similar arrangement that would pay him $195 million as a severance gift should he leave the company. Gillan has found a perfect alignment between her skills and values and the Cause of CalPERS. Says Gillan, concerned that a complacent Disney board had rubber-stamped these deals, "Disney is a prime example of why the current definition of independent boards isn't working."[30] Kayla Gillan is growing and learning and aligning her Calling more closely with the Cause of CalPERS' every day. Stride Rite's Chief Financial Officer, John M. Kelliher, says, "Of course, we'd rather not be on the list in the first place. But we have a good working relationship with Kayla — she's put a lot of time into understanding our company."

The greatest leaders in history worked closely with parceners to ensure that they had found their true Calling. Once this was confirmed, they helped them to increase their mastery, by helping them to grow, stretch and tackle extraordinary opportunities, often before they were fully ready. These are transformative leaders; leaders who change people. They are leaders who reveal the Inspirational Leader that lies within others. Doug Upchurch, former Executive Director of the Information Technology Training Association in Austin, Texas, says, "I am a teacher at heart — and teachers love seeing the light bulbs going on. Seeing people's lives changed for the better is very exciting. I love affecting employees' careers, and knowing what this can do for their families. This is more than teaching knowledge; we are seeing lives changed."

I worked for an Inspirational Leader at Manpower Limited. Jim Scheinfeld trusted me to run an entire business when I was just a twenty-seven-year-old rookie. He spent the next fourteen years teaching, encouraging, supporting, and, when necessary, defending — and always inspiring — me. The gift he gave me was the feeling that I have never worked a day in my life because I have always known and followed my Calling, I have loved the people I have worked with, and I have always aligned my Calling with a Cause. After fourteen years, Jim left, and a new chairman took over, who had different values and no clear and magnetic Cause. For the first time in years, I felt that my Calling was no longer aligned with a Cause I believed in, and therefore I was no longer inspired. Sadly, this could not be resolved and I resigned. But Jim's gifts to me as an Inspirational Leader were not lost because I had experienced the bliss that comes from aligning my Calling with a Cause, and to this day I have never settled for anything less.

Many people could not describe the Cause of their organization. This may be because a Cause has yet to be articulated and only tired mission, vision, and values statements are being substituted for the passion of a Cause. Or perhaps no attempt has been made to identify the Calling of the parceners, so they can align their Calling with the Cause. Or perhaps the leaders have deliberately avoided giving detailed communications of their real purposes, knowing that self-serving goals fail to inspire parceners.

The Terminator Seed

Monsanto Corp., whose corporate motto is "Food — Health — Hope," is one of the world's leading biotechnology companies and a pioneer in the development and production of genetically engineered seeds. They manufacture pest- and herbicide-resistant seeds for a variety of crops from corn to canola. For tens of thousands of years, farmers the world over have planted seeds, harvested their crops, saving some for seed to replant in the fall. To ensure a revenue stream for Monsanto's expensive research, the company has asked farmers not to do this, even requiring them to sign agreements to this effect, arguing that they need the revenues from new seed purchases to make such research financially viable. But farmers are not easily persuaded to follow these urgings, especially in developing countries. So Monsanto has developed a plan to ensure that farmers do things their way. The company has designed a new strain of chemically reengineered seeds that produce a healthy crop, but after they mature, the seeds they carry will become sterile and unable to reproduce. Critics of these tactics have built a movement, fuelled by the Internet, naming these genes *Terminator*, and making dark predictions about seed monopolies, bankrupt subsistence farmers, and toxic clouds of pollen drifting from these "super seeds" that might result in irreversible sterilization of great tracts of natural vegetation.[31]

Regardless of the arguments in this case, it raises questions of leadership such as "What is the Cause at Monsanto?" Is it about "Food — Health — Hope," helping to feed the world, improving the lives of farmers and liberating the poor, or about increasing shareholder value, raising the share price, overwhelming the competition, and dominating market share? Parceners are rarely inspired by greed or selfish aims for very long. To inspire parceners over the long term, leaders need to ensure that the Cause is rooted in something higher than self-interest, something beyond personal or corporate gain, something that recognizes and invokes a higher purpose. Inspiration is created when parceners understand how their Calling fits and serves this higher purpose, and how this alignment will resonate for them. Inspiration is a perfect fit between Calling and Cause.

Making the Connection

Some years ago, I was the president of Manpower Limited, part of what has today become the largest employer in the world. In those early pioneering days, a group of us were committed to building one of the most people-centered, inspirational, and soulful businesses in the world. One of the reasons we became so successful was our total commitment to people and to honoring their Calling. Instead of hiring "skills" — branch manager, controller, technical director, and so on — we simply committed to building the best team in the world. We knew that if we found inspired, talented people with a strong commitment to spirit and values, we would be able to build successful businesses around them. It was the spirit and the values we were building, not a series of tasks or an agglomeration of functions.

One day, an ex-helicopter pilot contacted us. He had heard about our Cause and wanted to be part of our dreams. As we got to know him, we knew that he would be a terrific human being to add to our team, and we agreed that we would all love to work together — but we weren't quite sure how. So we asked him what his Calling was. He told us he loved to fly and that he was a gifted pilot. We liked him so much, and fortunately he felt the same way about us, that we invited him to become a member of our organization. Of course, we had no idea what he would be doing! So we began to brainstorm ideas to align his Calling with our Cause. He explained that he had been flying personnel between the mainland of Scotland and the North Sea oilrigs during the booming development phase of the North Sea oil industry. He explained that there were now many companies in this business. With his expert advice, we put a plan together that resulted in the formation of a new company to maintain the helicopter fleets servicing the oilrigs. He became the president of the new operation, and it became one of our most successful businesses.

We repeated this approach many times during my fourteen years with the organization. We found many wonderful *people* — not functions — who were drawn to our Cause, and helped them to align their Calling with our Cause so they could create magical careers for themselves while, at the same time, investing their passion in our Cause. We became the largest truck-driving organization in the country; we helped to design some of the most important arterial highways in the nation; and we pioneered information technology testing and training. When the U.K. converted its currency from pounds, shillings, and pence into a decimal system, we took all the checks from the clearing banks and sorted them in London's Albert Hall, in the largest logistics operation ever undertaken in the country, thus averting any potential currency disruptions. The company became an international case study and an exemplar for people-centered growth and Values-centered Leadership™. And the organization was wildly profitable.

Recently I addressed an audience of 1,100 engineers at Pratt & Whitney, makers of the jet engines that power over half the commercial airlines in the world. I asked them if they put their heart and soul into their engines. Since I ride on their jet engines more than four hundred times a year, I had more than a passing interest in this matter. I told them that it would greatly comfort me to know that each engine is invested with the spirit of each parcener — rather like Japanese house-builders who carve their initials with pride into the beams of buildings, even though the buyer will never see them. I would feel differently about those engines if I knew they were not just the result of Pratt & Whitney's famed engineering genius, but also of each parcener's loving care. What I learned from Pratt & Whitney people is that they consider every passenger riding on their jet engines as a precious, sacred being and are therefore inspired to build the best jet engines in the world. This is Inspirational Leadership® at work and an inspiring confirmation for a frequent flyer like me!

Releasing the Music within Us

I run a virtual consulting organization. The first question we ask prospective consultants who wish to become certified in our work is "What is your Calling?" Some people are afraid to own up to their heart's inner yearning, and therefore die with their music still within them, intimidated, afraid or unaware, and missing the opportunity to live the uniqueness within. But we press them for their truth. One very successful management consultant privately longed to be a classical pianist, but was afraid to reveal this in a "business setting." He felt that there would be no application for his talent in a bottom-line world. I told the consultant of my experience years ago, when I attended a workshop in which a pianist trained at the Juilliard School of Music sat down in front of a grand piano and gave a virtuoso performance of Franz Liszt's *Liebsträume No. 3* in A flat minor. Then he rose and addressed the audience. The audience applauded his talented performance. But his mission was business as well as music.

"Liszt was an entrepreneur," he began. "He wrote music that was impossible to play on anything that had been invented at that time. His music was simply too fast for keyboard instruments of the day. So the contemporary music industry created one for him. It became known as the pianoforte, and later as the piano — an instrument designed to play at the speed that Liszt imagined in his mind. In the middle of the nineteenth century, Liszt's genius and inventiveness energized an entire industry — just as entrepreneurial genius does today. These days, software developers write programs for which no hardware has been written — hardware and microprocessor manufacturers respond to these entrepreneurial challenges with new machines and chips. Entrepreneurship and creativity always determine market directions, not the other way around."

By using the analogy of a musical genius, the speaker was able to make his point vividly and in an entertaining way that the audience would never forget. He showed that Liszt was not fazed by the limitations of available technology. He thought outside the box. I explained to this consultant that if being a pianist was his dream — the uniqueness within him that was calling to be lived — why couldn't he think outside the box, too? We could use his skills to teach values and spirituality in the workplace, if he was moved to align his Calling in service of our Cause.

Music hath caught a higher pace than any virtue that I know. It is the arch-reformer; it hastens the sun to its setting; it invites him to its rising; it is the sweetest reproach, a measured satire.

HENRY DAVID
THOREAU

Inspirational Leader Bonnie Wesorick of CPM Resources in Grand Rapids, Michigan, shows how nothing should be forced when aligning Calling and Cause. She says, "All I do is invite people to join me in important work. That is the reason why people have joined our organization. Doing work around what matters the most is what inspires people; when the work is purposeful and speaks to the heart and soul, people are present and inspired. Our work brings us to many different people; I invited them to be a part of the work. I show them how their presence would help it to become even more meaningful."

This approach is not always without its challenges. Bonnie describes a situation where a person came to work at CPM who was in the fast track of her career, which involved power struggles. "Her ultimate goal was to be an executive. I said, 'Here's the nature of our work.' People outside our organization asked her why she would want to work here, saying, 'Why do that, there is no position of power?' This helped her to think through what was important to her. After she became part of our work, she said there was a part of her she had never discovered. She wanted to bring her poetry to transform work cultures. Today she is one of my closest colleagues. She's a very different person now that she has aligned her Calling with our Cause. She is at peace, uses her wisdom, and touches people's hearts and souls. She also writes and shares her poetry with clients." Bonnie Wesorick sums up her philosophy this way, "I believe that work is a choice of how to bring the gifts of self to the world." As a result, the work Bonnie's organization does is changing the world. "We create workplaces that allow people to become human and still have the work done by the end of the shift. I was raised in a loving home environment. The philosophy in our family was that the integrity of the home would ensure the integrity of the workplace. For me, now, I believe the integrity of the workplace is molding the integrity of the homes. Working Moms and Dads are bringing home their lessons from the workplace. This has major implications for home and work."

Understanding Our Gifts

In my book *Reclaiming Higher Ground*, I argue that *mastery* is one of the Primary Values of outstanding leaders.[32] I define mastery as "Undertaking whatever you do, to the highest standards of which you are capable." A bonus for practitioners of mastery is that if they do it better than anyone else, they and others will reap handsome rewards. It is a wonderful law of life. If you play tennis better than anyone else, like Steffi Graf, or hockey like Wayne Gretzky, or dance like Nureyev or Karen Kain, sing like Pavarotti — or if you lead like Jim Paquette of the Sisters of Charity of Leavenworth, Mark Scott of Mid-Columbia Medical Center, the late Bill Gore of W. L. Gore Inc., Cal Turner of Dollar General Stores, Caroline Martin of Riverside Health System, Yvon Chouinard of Patagonia, Dave Duffield of PeopleSoft, Bill Pollard of ServiceMaster, Bonnie Wesorick of CPM Resources, William George of Medtronic, Inc., John Mackey of Whole Foods Markets, David Page of Fairview Health Services, Jack Lowe of TD Industries, or Anita Roddick of The Body Shop — not only will you accumulate spiritual and material wealth, but the energy of your talent will create opportunities and jobs for others.

Leveraging Our Talents

We sometimes forget what our real gifts are and become distracted or unfocused, and this causes us to become confused about how we apply the magic of our Calling in the service of others. Sometimes the processes of our work, what we make, or the functions we provide — the means in other words — become confused with the ends — why we do what we do. The ends, our Cause, are far more important than the means with which we achieve them.

Some years ago, one of Manpower Limited's quarterly board meetings was being held quite close to Christmas. As the president of the company, I took advantage of the opportunity to present a proposal to engage us very directly in our community. The centerpiece of my suggestion was that we personally visit less fortunate families in the major urban areas in which we operated to deliver Christmas dinners to them.

The reaction to my proposal surprised me. The senior executive responsible for day-to-day operations raised his eyebrows and peered at me intently. "Are you crazy?" he asked.

What do you say to someone who asks if you are crazy after you have just suggested an act of generosity? I mumbled something in an effort to buy time while I collected my thoughts.

He looked me squarely in the eyes as he chided me: "We have built a business from scratch that today employs 72,000 people — ten years ago, those jobs didn't even exist. In all probability, each of those 72,000 people has at least one dependant and one friend. Therefore, the jobs we have created are directly or indirectly benefiting the lives of over 200,000 people. Creating over 70,000 new jobs is the finest work we could do for our community. Why would we divert our talent from this good work to something for which we are untrained and unprepared?"

He had a point.

Most of us want to support charities, and it is good that we do so. But it is not the only way to give. If leadership is your Calling and your greatest mastery, then it may be a better gift than cash because it can be leveraged into so much more. The most precious gift of all is your time and talent, and in sharing it, we share our best with others. As Lao-tzu said in the sixth century BC, "Give a man a fish, and you feed him for a day. Teach a man to fish, and you feed him for a lifetime."

Ever since my colleague taught me this lesson, I have politely declined requests for cash donations to charities. In my particular case (and I am not saying this is the same for everyone), giving money is like giving the fish. Whatever small talent I possess lies in leading organizations and inspiring others, and I am more than prepared to share these gifts and my time for a worthwhile Cause.

A great concert pianist might be asked to donate a day's income to charity, but the charity would gain more if they received the gift of her time and talent for a day. With this gift, they could organize a charity concert and collect all of the gate and box office receipts. The contribution by the great concert pianist remains the same but, through leveraging, the benefit to the charity is far greater.

The pursuit of mastery in the service of humanity is one of the greatest contributions we can make on this planet. The lesson is to be aware of our gifts and to share them in the best interests of others, to leverage them as strongly as possible. In this way, our Calling becomes our joy, because it becomes joyful for others and aligned with a Cause.

Being on a Dream Team

None of us can completely insulate ourselves from the turbulence of the marketplace. Change and chaos are an unavoidable fact of life. However, we all have the power to select the kinds of teams we belong to — and that is what most of us try to do. It makes sense to be on a team that is potent and fun, rather than one that is dysfunctional. Then we can ride these waves of change safely. Often we are too heavy to take off. Dream teams are light enough to fly.

Finding a dream team, then, that meets our spiritual aspirations is vital for the soul because without it, we become spiritually adrift. Such alienation often afflicts people at work, just as much as the realization that they have yet to find their Calling. In fact, though it may not be an inspiring experience, many people can subsist with relative comfort on a dream team, even though they may not yet have found their Calling. For a while, the sense of community offsets the emptiness that comes from not having a vocation.

I mentioned earlier the term *Sanctuary*, which comes from the Latin *sanctus*, "sacred, holy place"; it is a place of refuge or protection, a shelter, as a soulful workplace, a safe environment. We may not be able to change the world around us, but we can change ourselves. In this way, though the world around us may be crazy or dangerous, in the Sanctuary of our own space, we are secure. A Sanctuary is like a Teflon shield, repelling the toxicity around us. But a Sanctuary is not a physical location (I prefer to think of that as a Soulspace), it is an attitude. Sanctuaries are often formed by groups of like-minded individuals who seldom meet, but share values, love, trust and who respect each other and enjoy a common code. A Sanctuary is a holy place, a place where we give reverence to all of the people and things within it. It is a place where we practice a sacred code, live in grace, and honor each other.[33]

A dream team is a Sanctuary. We each have the tools and the opportunity to bring our own influence upon our team, shaping its character with our own, and adding and strengthening its values and spiritual fiber. It is because of this spiritual energy that a team becomes a *Sanctuary* — a team that stands together on higher ground.

Often, though, we are faced with some tough choices. The team we belong to or the organization or community with whom we are associated is so toxic that we cannot align ourselves with its values or practices, or with the Cause. Spiritual liberation will not be ours until this dilemma is addressed — either the team changes or we do. Often this leaves us with only one practical option: we must sever our ties with the dysfunctional people and organizations that drain our energy and sap our soul of its potential. This, sadly, is sometimes the only route to authenticity, to ensure that we stop living the lie of a career where the money is good, but the spiritual rewards are non-existent. To remain in these circumstances is purgatory on Earth. Pathogenic behavior does not inspire and it is injurious to the soul.

When We Must Part

Occasionally, there is a need for us to accept the sad truth that the Calling of one person does not easily support the Cause of another. Mature organizations deal with these situations with grace, ensuring that the needs of the soul are always appropriately addressed. The opposite, of course, often goes by the euphemisms of *re-engineering* and *downsizing*.

Some years ago a top 10 Fortune company asked me to help them to communicate from the heart the impending layoffs flowing from their massive downsizing program. I spent many weeks with top management, philosophizing, debating, scripting, designing, and encouraging empathy. At the end of it all, an elaborate, compassionate program was developed with all of top management fanning out across the country to deliver the unhappy news personally, in a loving and values-centered way, to all of the people affected. But on the appointed day, they just could not do it. They simply could not bring themselves to speak the compassionate and caring words I had asked them to believe, feel and say. I had not just asked them to speak the words; I had asked them to act in a compassionate and caring way, too. But the senior vice-president said to me on the eve of the road show, "Lance, we are engineers, we just cannot say or do this." So they abandoned my plan and fanned out into the affected offices supported by an outplacement firm, where they delivered a message that roughly went like this: "You are fired. Please step across the hall, where an outplacement consultant will take care of you. Thank you for your contribution. Have a nice day." The effect on employees was absolutely devastating. The survivors were so shocked by the callousness to which their former colleagues were subjected that morale and productivity slumped across the entire organization. An exodus of some of the finest people in the company was also triggered for several years following.

Contrast this with the strategy of Levi Strauss and Co. In November 1997, CEO Robert Haas announced the layoff of 6,395 employees (34% of its U.S. and Canadian workforce) and the closure of eleven factories. With this he announced an unprecedented $200 million employee benefits program to help the employees affected through the transition. Each employee received three weeks' pay for each year of service, eight weeks' pay from the date of the announcement, plus counseling services. Employees were entitled to the package even if they found a new position immediately. The company paid for health care benefits for eighteen months and up to $6,000 per employee for education, job training, or moving expenses. The Levi Strauss Foundation granted $8 million over three years to the eight communities affected to ease the social and economic impact of the closures.

If there are really no options left but separation, that is, if more imaginative options are beyond the grasp of the organization's leaders, then let's separate in a graceful, caring, and friendly way that honors the souls of those affected and treats them as sacred beings.

9

Step Five

Serving Parceners

After achieving pure clarity about their Destiny, defining and championing the Cause, reaffirming their commitment to their own Calling, and coaching others to find and master theirs and then aligning that Calling with the Cause, **the Inspirational Leader asks the parcener, "How may I serve you?"** More than anything else, parceners yearn for leaders who genuinely seek to serve them, for this is a signal of love — and love inspires.

Service is the *raison d'être* of the Aquarian leader archetype. It is in serving others that *we best serve ourselves*. Once they have defined their Destiny, their Cause, and their Calling, and have aligned it with the Cause, then Inspirational Leaders ask parceners, "How may I serve you?" More than anything else, parceners yearn for leaders who genuinely seek to serve them, since this is a signal of love — and love inspires.

A new model of Servant-leadership is emerging based on sharing, co-operating, and consideration. In this new story thinking, life is not a continuous improvement project in which leaders strive endlessly towards greater and greater personal achievements. Instead they choose to ask others, "How may I serve you?"

> You derive your supreme satisfaction not from your ability to amass things or to achieve superficial power but from your ability to identify yourselves with others and to share fully in their needs and hopes. In short, for fulfillment, we look to identification, rather than acquisition.
>
> NORMAN COUSINS

Once, working with a client who was the CEO of a very large dental practice, I gave this advice: "Tomorrow morning, please open your management meeting by asking everyone the following question: 'How may I serve you?' You may feel a little odd, even awkward, but please just try it and see what happens." Later that morning, he called me to report on the outcome. He said, "You should have seen the looks on their faces…their jaws all dropped, and they just stared at me. They had never heard me say anything like this in their lives before. I always *wanted* something *from* them. Here I was offering to serve them. They were stunned. Afterwards, they told me that it had the effect of completely changing the dynamics and the chemistry of the team. It was amazing."

Inspirational Leaders serve parceners in tangible and intangible ways. Inspirational Leader Cal Turner of Dollar General Stores gives this example:

In order to create a true financial partnership with store managers, we extended company stock options in 1998 to store managers and assistant store managers in every store. After they have been working with us for two years, they become eligible to receive stock options. I know of no other retailer in the world who does that. This is smart and is reflective of our values. These people are often neglected by retailers and retail management, but our partners know we care about them when we do this. Inspirational Leaders put their stock where their mouth is.

Sometimes I sit in at the beginning of our personal review discussions. Once, during a review with a junior but long-serving employee, he began the review by saying, "I want to thank you for my Dollar General house. Thanks to the stock options, my family lives in a house we never would have been able to. My wife and I thank you." As this employee talked about the people in his department, he showed that he was clearly committed to his team and had developed a strong commitment to those persons who follow him.

The Ideal Parent: The Ultimate Servant-Leader

One of the prevailing role models in our society is the parent, and often we experience the parent/child relationship as one characterized by power and control, permissions and requests, giving and taking. The result is that many of us are orphans — our parents don't know who we are. The corporation, the employer, the government, the law enforcement officer, the educator and physician occupy a similar "parent" role, in which we expect them to provide control, exert their power, and have the answers, but not

> **The servant-leader is servant first. It begins with the natural feeling that one wants to serve. Then conscious choice brings one to aspire to lead. The difference manifests itself in the care taken by the servant first to make sure that other people's highest priority needs are being served. The best test, and the most difficult to administer is: do those served grow as persons, do they while being served become healthier, wiser, freer, more autonomous, more likely themselves to become servants?**
>
> FROM *THE SERVANT AS LEADER*, BY ROBERT K. GREENLEAF

really know us. Perhaps we have been drawing the wrong conclusions and learning the wrong lessons from the role model of our parents.

Somewhere deep in our hearts, we never lose the need to be cared for. If I think about some of the moments of pure joy in my life, many are associated with being nurtured — as when someone defends me, spoils me, bakes me a cake, gives me a hug, tells me a story, cares about me when I am unwell, or straightens my clothing. Do we ever "mature" to the point where we become indifferent to the magic ministrations of a caring soul? Is there not an important lesson for us here? Should we not all learn a little of the magic of mothers and fathers?

At their best, parents offer unconditional love, consistent communications, support, loyalty, and commitment to parceners, even as they impose discipline and order. They create community and bonding among "family." They promote growth and development, health and safety, ethics and morality, beauty and comfort, nourishment and balance, spirit and values. They inspire and teach, always in a loving way. They are boosters who cheer and encourage. The hug and serve. They make peace. They provide wisdom, vision, and hope. This suggests that the ideal parental model may be the first and best example of Servant-leadership that each of us can experience. What greater characteristics could we be looking for in a leader?

People Whisperers

Real animal lovers have never believed in the theories of Ivan Petrovich Pavlov (1849–1936), the Russian physiologist and Nobel laureate, best known for his studies of reflex behavior. He became famous for his linear theory of motivation: punish failure until it stops and reward success in order to encourage its repetition. Over the years, Pavlovian philosophy has evolved into a kind of metatheory. Most animal training is based on this principle, as are most corporate reward and compensation systems. Most leadership theories also follow this superficial and misguided philosophy, and nearly all motivational theories follow similar lines.

Those who enjoyed a loving bond with their pets have always sensed that these harsh techniques might be right for the teacher, but not for the student. Smacking a dog when it piddles on the rug is not a Buddha-like, loving action. To the sensitive ears of a dog, a swat on the head with a folded newspaper is the human equivalent of a whack on the side of the head with a two-by-four. Few sensitive beings, whether they have two legs or four, relish having a folded newspaper scrunched in their ears every time they displease another.

Similarly, violent techniques are frequently used to train horses. Horrifying though it may be to some, horses are "broken" by blindfolding them, hitting and whipping them, lassoing their feet and tying them to stakes — all in an attempt to *break their spirit.* Cowboy heroes are called broncobusters.

This paradigm of motivation isn't what happens in a loving relationship. Let's look at the maternal model of Servant-leadership for a moment. When a baby is learning to walk, we do not punish it. If a baby falls over, we don't say, "Boy, you're dumb. I don't think you're going to get this. I'm not sure you have the potential to be a good walker. I'm going to give you one more chance and then you're toast! Now, get with it!" When your toddler first tries to raise herself from the floor and collapses after two paces, you pick her up, dust her off, tell her how beautiful and wonderful she is, that you love her, and then start all over again. Parents repeat this process in a loving, supportive way until they, and their children, are rewarded with those momentous "baby's first steps." We praise them and love them, speak to their souls, and hug them until they get it. This successful system is based on love, not on the fear-drenched, carrot-and-stick formulae of Pavlov. Children who grow up in such a nurturing and supportive culture become whole adults. My wife and I are excellent examples of this theory. Her adoring parents praised her to success, whereas I was alternately rewarded and kicked around by mine, depending on how well I met their ever-increasing demands. Both my wife and I love our parents, but from my perspective, my struggles to shed the baggage I accumulated in my early life have seemed, to me at least, harder than hers. When my wife came home with straight "As" and one "B," her parents praised her and encouraged her. When I did the same, my parents scolded me for the errant "B." Though I loved my parents, it has taken me decades to realize that I do not have to be perfect by someone else's yardstick in order to be a complete and spiritual human. This was just an example of Pavlovian theory being transferred to child-raising — very common at that time and still true for the majority of leaders.

Success is the ability to go from failure to failure with no loss of enthusiasm.

WINSTON S. CHURCHILL

We don't have to be slaves to the Pavlovian concept of motivation or leadership. There is a better model for our age, based on the work of *horse whisperers*. This is the age-old technique that favors silent communication and physical cues to teach and communicate with horses. Horse whisperers train through hand gestures and body movements, instead of yanking on the reins, or using spurs and whips. They use touch and gesture to create a spiritual connection with a horse, sending a clear message of love. This enables a horse whisperer to take a wild stallion into a barn and emerge two hours later with a rideable mount.

Horse whispering has gained much publicity in recent years, following the publication of Monty Roberts' book, *The Man who Listens to Horses*, and the release of the Robert Redford movie, *The Horse Whisperer*. As a result, the old story of horse training is slowly changing. We need the same thing to happen with people.

We need *people* whisperers.

The old story of leadership and training, and the old way of getting a horse to accept a saddle and rider was to break its spirit — Arian and Piscean leadership. A horse whisperer is an Aquarian leader archetype who avoids bribing a horse or cheating it of food, and instead copies and perfects the actions of the matriarchal mare who causes the other horses to yield when moving through their midst.

Kent Williamson, a horse whisperer from Millarville, Alberta, says, "If a person leads a horse by pulling or forcing, the horse learns from day one to resist pressure and go against it. From then on, you always have to make the horse do things, as opposed to asking and maybe receiving, through willingness." Monty Roberts, from Solvang, California, argues that no one has the right to say "You must or I will hurt you" to any other creature.

This includes humans. We need to cause the behavior we seek through love. This requires us to communicate in a way that empathizes with others, by communicating spiritually with them and giving spiritual power to them — the Aquarian leader in action. The result is an act of conspiracy — from *con*, which means with, and *spirare*, which means to breathe — to breathe together. Conspiring together is to serve each other, as horse whisperers do when truly serving the needs of the horse by conspiring with them. We truly breathe together, so that we both grow towards our full potential.

Williamson demonstrates this philosophy as he moves his body towards one of the pressure points of a horse, its hip, to cause the animal to step away. When he turns to walk, the animal follows. It is about engaging the spirit, not breaking it. As Monty Roberts puts it, "The object of the teacher is to create an environment in which the student can learn."

Nothing is so strong as gentleness, and nothing is so gentle as true strength.

RALPH STOCKMAN

This new logic of gentleness over violence has inspired the U.S. Bureau of Land Management to set up a program in four states called Wild Horse Inmate Programs (WHIPs). When prison inmates learn and experience the techniques of horse whispering, coaching wild stallions with love and sensitivity instead of aggression and violence, they often hold this attitude for the rest of their lives. If hardened criminals can be transformed this way, replacing terror with trust and shedding their violent habits in favor of relationships built on compassion and caring, then so can our leaders, in the corporate sector or other arenas.

From myself, I am copper, Through you, friend, I am gold; From myself I am a stone, But through you I am a gem.

RUMI

Michael is serving his third prison term at the Susanville, California, correctional center, this time with a twenty-month sentence for possession of methamphetamines and assaulting a police officer. "You've got to take your time [with a horse]," he says. "I was kind of nervous when I first got out here. But you can't win a fight with a wild horse. They'll kill you first." The spiritual connection he has made with horses has deeply affected him.

"This is about as good as it gets for me," he says. "I've learned a lot here, and I like getting off the prison yard. Every horse I've trained I'd like to take home with me." A plumber by training, Michael plans to work with horses when he is released, perhaps owning a horse and doing some training.

We may respect a leader, but the ones we love are servant-leaders. They are the ones who teach with love and who learn and grow with us, listen and empathize, and honor us from deep within their souls — thus making a spiritual connection between leader and parcener — they are people whisperers.

Like Inspirational Leadership®, horse whispering is taught through experience, by apprenticing with masters, as I did with Jim Scheinfeld, who was my servant-leader. It is a gift that is passed on, like the wisdom of elders. One of the dozen horse whisperers in North America is Buck Brannaman of Sheridan, Wyoming, who learned from another horse whisperer named Ray Hunt, who teaches "thinking harmony with horses" at his horse clinic in Ribera, New Mexico. In turn, Hunt's own mentor was a legendary master teacher named Tom Dorrance, who still teaches a technique he calls "true unity," the willing communication between horse and human. Notice how all these techniques and metaphors transfer so easily to people. Instead of saying "the willing communication between horse and human," we could just as easily say "the willing communication between human and human."

Another observation worthy of note about many horse whisperers is their domestic background. It may be more than mere coincidence that Brannaman, Hunt, and Dorrance all come from abusive backgrounds ranging from alcoholism to beating, violence, and abandonment. The personal experience of these three legendary horse whisperers has perhaps informed their philosophy of life and leadership — they learned the hard way that there is a better way. Monty Roberts' father, Marvin, a Salinas, California, horse trainer, hit him with stable chains and dominated horses with similarly rough treatment. "I believed there was a better way," said Roberts, and he decided to find it.

Growing up in Whitehall, Montana, Brannaman says, "I was always kind of scared of my dad. He was pretty mean to us boys. I remember we'd come home from school for lunch, and my mom would drop me off at school again on the way to work. She was a waitress in a town about fifty miles away, and my dad had a shoe repair and saddle shop in town. I remember from about eight or nine years old, I would beg her not to go to work every day, 'cause I was terrified of being at home alone with my dad for the four or five hours after school, before she'd get home."

A domestic heritage of violence, aggression, punishment, control, and abuse of power can result in different lessons. Many leaders carry forward the cellular memory of their familial experiences and convert them into models for running their organizations. Their experiences are stored as anger, which is released as violence and aggression — their shadow. This results in organizations that are as dysfunctional as their families were — their leadership philosophies are the same. Many people recognize the pathologies of their families in their organizations, having seen and experienced them in their earlier lives.

Other leaders take the same experiences and convert them into different lessons. One of the leaders who loomed large in my early career was as paranoid as anyone I have known. He even hired a private detective to report on the off-work activities of my sales team. But I learned *what not to do* from this teacher. There are lessons to be learned from every experience.

Some horse trainers have imported their macho experiences into their work — these are the bronco-busters. Horse whisperers have learned a different lesson from the same experiences. They have learned that horses should be "started" not "broken" because an intelligent horse has as much to teach us as we have to teach it. This is the heritage of horse whispering handed down from Tom Dorrance to Ray Hunt and Buck Brannaman. As Ray Hunt puts it, "You're not working on the horse, you're working on yourself." Years ago, Ray Hunt asked Tom Dorrance where he'd learned his skills. Dorrance replied, "Ray, I learned it from the horse." This is universal wisdom. We learn it from the parcener.

The metaphor of the horse whisperer transfers easily to the servant-leader. Aquarian leaders transfer power to the parcener, as a horse whisperer does to a horse. The result is a union, which is a magical thing to observe.

This expression of honoring that horse whisperers and people whisperers make to each other by serving is vital. We each need to know that others regard us as sacred. Within my organization's worldwide network called the Higher Ground Community, which I referred to earlier, we have a tradition of greeting each other with the Hindi greeting, *Namaste!* It is hard to translate exactly, but here is an approximate definition:

N A M A S T E !
I honor the place in you where the entire Universe resides,
I honor the place in you of love, of light, of truth, of peace.
I honor the place within you where,
If you are in that place in you
And I am in that place in me,
There is only one of us!

Each time we meet, or when we write to each other, we include this blessing — a declaration of respect, honoring the sacredness of each other. We are trying to be people whisperers.

"How Can I Be Kind, Instead of Right?"

Next time you are engaged in a heated discussion with a supplier, customer, or colleague, pause for a moment and ask yourself the quintessential question of the Aquarian leader: "How can I be kind, instead of right?"

Being right serves the ego; being kind serves the soul. Being right serves me; being kind serves us. Being kind inevitably leads us to the question, "How may I serve you?"

Serving others and practicing loving kindness is not the first image that springs to mind when we think about corporate executives or leaders of organizations. This may be because we train aggression into contemporary leaders. When Cornell University asked 250 business school students what traits they thought made a great leader, they put being "results-oriented" at the top of their list, and 60% said they admired slash-and-burn downsizers like "Chainsaw" Al Dunlap.[34] American Airlines is one of the best airlines in America, and Robert Crandall, American's former CEO, is often hailed as the savior of the airline industry, the inventor of frequent flier programs (the AAdvantage Awards Program in 1981), and the man who pioneered the renaissance of air travel. Inside the company, he was better known as "Fang" or "Darth Vader."[35] Jack Welch, the chief executive officer of General Electric Co., has been routinely ranked as the most admired and respected executive in America. He was voted "most respected" CEO in four of the last five *Industry Week* Annual CEO Surveys.[36] At the same time, he is also notorious among those who know him for his toughness and profanity. *Fortune* magazine recently reported that Jack Welch "conducts meetings so aggressively that people tremble. He attacks almost physically with his intellect — criticizing, demeaning, ridiculing, humiliating." During his seventeen-year reign as CEO, Welch, a.k.a. "Neutron Jack," has re-engineered over 150,000 people from their jobs in his relentless pursuit to be number one or two in every market segment in which GE operates. In his biography, *At Any Cost: Jack Welch, General Electric and the Pursuit of Profit*, Thomas F. O'Boyle describes GE as a company "managed by threat and intimidation rather than encouragement."[37]

When we pay tribute to the characteristics of violence and intimidation, celebrating them as exemplary leadership qualities, what message are we sending current and future leaders? What kind of model are we encouraging them to follow? In the case of American Airlines, the numerous labor disputes endured by the company suggest that old story leadership inevitably contributes to the paradox of our times — profits are up, but people are down.

Serving Parceners by Listening

I recently told an audience of nearly fifteen hundred people that if I ever become King of the Universe, I will abolish all performance appraisal systems, which are universally reviled, by both the appraisers and the appraisees. Often, their main purpose is to serve as instruments of power and control over others. I added that since organizational theorists have encouraged us to separate the performance appraisal from the salary review, this is a practice now followed by most organizations, yet few people are naïve enough to believe that a poor appraisal will not be reflected in a subsequent salary review. The audience erupted into spontaneous applause (a frequent reaction whenever I make this observation), which then swelled into a standing ovation. At the half-time break, the managers of the organization pulled me aside for a huddle. "This organization has just hired expensive consultants who overhauled our performance appraisal system, which we will be using for many years into the future, so we would appreciate it if you did not talk about new approaches and alternatives," they admonished me. I asked the manager if she realized that when fifteen hundred employees applaud, it represents clear research. They were sending a message that they disagreed with her. She shrugged, citing the need to be competitive, to increase performance, to reduce costs, to focus greater effort towards customers, and to not make leaders look like they were out of touch (which, I pointedly observed, they were!).

> **Sometimes you have to be silent in order to be heard.**
>
> WILMA ASKINAS

We serve best by listening and then acting constructively on what we have heard. We alienate people when we believe that "we know better than they do." Inspirational Leaders understand the wisdom I described earlier: employees are the customers of the leader — our job as Inspirational Leaders is to meet the needs of our customers/parceners, just as well as we have learned to meet the needs of our customers/buyers.

Bonnie Wesorick, the Inspirational Leader of CPM Resources in Grand Rapids, Michigan, says, "We serve parceners by tapping their gifts and connecting them with others to share their gifts. I honor their choice to serve. I ask, 'What would help you live what you believe?' I connect them to one another, and provide opportunities via gatherings to help them learn from and teach each other."

We can listen to ourselves, too, by asking ourselves questions and listening to the truth of our inner voices. We might ask: Is what I am doing inspiring others right now? If I were the other person, would I feel inspired by these words? If I say (or do) what I intend, will it inspire? Before I make my point, how can I be sure it inspires? Are my colleagues inspired? What inspires this person — how can I serve them? How will I live in order to inspire?

The Inspirational Leader as Mystic

We are better able to serve when we view each other with a sense of wonder, with the awareness that there exists within us all potential that is often not immediately apparent. Everyone is gifted and wondrous in their own special way, and Aquarian leaders trust in the potential of the Universe — which includes each other. Thus, Inspirational Leaders are mystics, because inspiration and mysticism are handmaidens. If we fail to see the beauty in each other, we fail to honor each other, and where there is no honor, there can be no inspiration. Seeing the beauty in others is to love them, and from love flows inspiration. Every person who is inspired is a person who is loved.

How shall we define a mystic? A mystic is a person who sees the wonder in all of life, all of the time. A mystic is a person who looks at a flower and marvels at the colors, the sheen, the geometry, the fragrance, the radiance, the poetry, and the love within. The beauty of life continuously confounds the mystic. For the mystic, there is wonder and beauty in every boulder, in the hollow of a hill, in the symphony of a songbird, in the crouch of a cat, in the hocks of a horse, in the contours of a cloud, in the shimmer of a star, in the surge of the surf, in the rhythm of a river, in the flourish of a phrase, in the jest in a joke,

I picked the rose in a hurry.
I was afraid of the Gardener.
Then I heard the soft voice of Him,
"What's the value of one rose?
I give you the whole garden."

RUMI

in the laugh of a lover. When presented with a glorious sunset, a rapturous symphony, a ravishing sonnet, or brilliant artistry, a mystic loses all sense of space and time. A mystic sees the wonder in the shadow side of life, too — in the slums, war zones, places of pestilence, and in the suffering that surrounds us. When we effortlessly connect with the wonder of life, savoring the ceaseless beauty of the Universe, then we merge with our soul, and therefore with God, becoming one with the Universe. This is the moment when God observes us. When we look at a blade of grass, a flower or tree, an insect, mammal, bird or fish, indeed, any natural thing, and especially each other, God is observing us through these proclamations of life. When we watch the wonders of the world, we are watching God watch us. This is the moment when we become mystics. It is in this instant that we become woven seamlessly into the fabric of the Universal Consciousness. It is in this moment that we see the beauty, the potential, the marvel and the soul of every person. This is the moment when we breathe with God — this is the divine moment when we become inspired and therefore are inspiring.

Love is a canvas furnished by Nature and embroidered by imagination.

VOLTAIRE

The corporate mystic sees life as play, not work. Nature does not engage in work — it indulges in play. If we were to look upon the activities of nature as work, they would become dismal and boring, in the same way that work appears boring to a lot of people. But by looking at the activities of nature, or the activities of our work, as play, they become filled with wonder — mystical. This is a concept that corporate mystics carry into their work lives, and the difference in the energy they create around themselves is palpable as a result.

To be a mystic, we must accept others as they are, honoring them as sacred, rather than assessing them from a place of judgment. Viewed this way, we will see each other as unique testimonies to the genius of God. God made no weeds, no runts, no losers, and no failures. We are all sacred, and each of us who stands in the light of another who views us this way will become inspired. When we are inspired, it is because we feel the unconditional love of another, hearing their advice as loving support, not criticism, and their teaching as healing wisdom. The Inspirational Leader, that is, someone who loves and is loved, creates an inspired partner who loves and is loved.

Inspirational Leaders like Caroline Martin, Executive Director of Riverside Health System, understand this oneness with a Supreme Being at a very deep level. She tells a story that makes this point:

I was supposed to relieve a baby-sitter who was caring for my grand-children and had to call to say I would be late. When I finally arrived home, the sitter said, "Kaitlyn (age 2) is asleep, but Kelsey (age 4) is still awake. She was upset when she couldn't talk with you on the phone." As I crawled into bed with Kelsey (who was pretending to be asleep), I asked her, "What makes you so special?" My granddaughter said, "Uhmm, God." To which I said, "I know God MADE you, but what is it about YOU that makes you so special?" She said, "Oh, my laughing heart." I said, "Your laughing heart?" And she replied, "Yes. You know, Bama, I was sad about not talking to you on the phone, but inside, my heart was still laughing."

To me, this was a renewed lesson that God lives in each of us, in our hearts, that the essence of our being is love. We then can remember that every set of circumstances and every relationship is an opportunity to give and receive that love. Everyone is full of love and laughter; being able to see and draw it from all those around you allows us to stay in the stream of LIFE. And, if you believe that God lives in everybody, then you have to respect everybody.

Spirit and Service: A Means and an End

Moral excellence, righteousness, goodness: these are the sweet sounds of virtue. She is the bond of all perfections and the heart of all life's satisfactions. Virtue makes men sensible, alert, understanding, wise, courageous, considerate, joyous, truthful, and visionary. Virtue is the sun of our lesser world, the sky of good conscience. She is so beautiful that she finds favor with both God and man. There is nothing lovely without her, for she is the essence of wisdom, and all else is folly. Greatness must be measured in terms of virtue, and not in terms of fortune. Virtue alone makes a man worth loving in life, and worth remembering after death.

BALTASAR GRACIAN

As leaders, when we talk of serving others, it is the intentions that count more than our words; what we do counts more than what we say. Parceners are more interested in our integrity than our speeches about integrity, and their antennae are sensitive and efficient to any possible incongruities. People whose souls have been trampled on at work yearn for leaders who are prepared to serve them. They want to know that when leaders have choices, the well-being of people comes before the bottom line.

Our preoccupation with increasing output, profits, market share,

> **Service is the rent each of us pays for living — the very purpose of life and not something you do in your spare time or after you have reached your personal goals.**
>
> MARIAN WRIGHT EDELMAN

productivity, stock prices, and other metrics — the ends — often clouds our judgment, causing us to overlook the lack of virtue in our means. The old story adage that the ends justify the means is seldom true. No ends are worthwhile if we must pursue shabby means to achieve them. Life is often a better measure than profit.

An example of Piscean, old story leadership is the latest rush by some executives to embrace the concept of "employability." Many corporate leaders are now suggesting that the guarantee of job security is anachronistic, having been replaced by a new sort of "contract" that requires employees to be responsible for their own career and skill development, thus remaining employable. For their part, companies see their role to provide career resources and opportunities for training. When layoffs occur, according to this reasoning, employees are protected by their ability to find alternative employment. In this proposition, employers declare that change is inevitable, that employees must prepare for it, and then unburden themselves of any shared responsibility. This is not leadership — it is abdication. Inspirational Leaders serve parceners by sharing information about economic prospects for the enterprise, helping them to grow and learn and guiding the mastery of their Calling. This is what helped Baptist Health Systems become number one in America in customer satisfaction. Imaginative leaders like Fred Smith of Federal Express and Donald F. Hastings of Lincoln Electric simply refuse to accept the inevitability of layoffs. "Thinking ahead and having creative solutions for when there is a downturn is what management is all about," asserts Hastings. When Pella Corp., a 3,500-employee-owned window manufacturer in Pella, Iowa, overhauled their company, they cut production times by two-thirds without any layoffs. Anand Sharma, who advised the company, said, "No one worried about losing their job, so [parceners] created change instead."[38] Aquarian Leaders hold humans as sacred and think in terms of serving them not throwing them away.

The APACHE Project

In the early 1980s, a team of U.S. researchers developed a project to measure the variables accounting for better survival rates among patients suffering from similar illnesses. Over a three-year period, the researchers collected data from thirteen major U.S. tertiary care hospitals covering 5,030 randomly selected acute care patients. All of the hospitals had similar technical capabilities in their intensive care units, but differing leadership styles for staffing, commitment to teaching, research, and education.

In the field of healthcare, there is a statistical method for determining the correlation between the severity of an illness and the statistical probability of death in each case. It is called Acute Physiology and Chronic Health Evaluation (APACHE). This system enables healthcare professionals to predict the likely outcome of survival against a large international sample.

In the analysis, one hospital had significantly better results (sixty-one predicted but forty-one observed deaths), while another had significantly worse results (58% more deaths than predicted). Technically, there was very little difference between the hospitals being studied. *The significant variable proved to be the quality of leadership.* What the researchers found in particular was that the better-performing hospitals achieved superior interpersonal dynamics among the intensive care unit staff. When leaders served their parceners well, the medical staff was able to serve their patients better. The researchers reported that "the degree of coordination of intensive care significantly influenced its effectiveness."[39]

A few years ago, I conducted a research project for the leading reinsurance company in the world. Our goal was to determine the reasons for the sustained loyalty of their top thirty clients. The presidents and top executives of these VIP clients were flown in from around the world and invited to a roundtable session in which they were asked some three hundred questions. Their responses were captured anonymously through the use of individual keypads connected directly to our proprietary computer systems. After the questions were answered, the findings were tallied instantly and then discussed frankly with the entire group. The company was one of the most sophisticated and technically advanced organizations in its field in the world, and justifiably proud of its huge investment in technical mastery. But when these major customers were asked why they continued to give the company so much business year after year, it was not the mastery they cited, but the relationships, the chemistry between key people in both organizations built up over time and nourished assiduously. The CEO of the company was passionate about creating deep relationships of the highest quality, both internally and externally — and it showed. Employees, suppliers, and customers loved him and the standards of leadership he continually demonstrated and encouraged.

Since it is now possible for any organization with similar investments to achieve the same levels of mastery and technical prowess as any other, the only *real* distinguishing feature between different organizations will be the quality of their leadership, which means how well leaders *serve* parceners, customers, suppliers, and their community. When I was a university professor, my MBA students would ask me which company would be the best for them to work for. I always gave the same advice: find a great leader to work for, not a company. Working for Michael Dell is not the same thing as working for Dell Computer. It's the same for suppliers, customers, and employees. Find a great leader to work for or do business with. Servant-leadership is the new (well, nothing is really new) competitive advantage.

Being committed to serving others is a virtuous practice because it is nearly always a spiritual one, *and* the most profitable practice in the long run. In other words, for the Aquarian leader, contrary to the perspective of the Arian leader, the means *always* determines the ends. This raises a number of practical questions. First, how do we ensure that our strategy flows from our values, rather than the other way around? Arian leaders begin with strategy and then adopt the values that fit. Aquarian leaders develop their unshakable values first, and then develop strategies that flow from them.

Give elaborate feasts, be gracious when entertaining and be generous to your guests.

THE WAY OF SUFI CHIVALRY (11TH CENTURY)

So before we invite parceners to co-develop and implement strategy, we must be comfortable with the spiritual underpinnings of our work. We need to ask difficult questions in order to test the mettle of our values: Are we pursuing noble values in our work? Does our work serve others at least as much as, if not more than, ourselves? Are we treading lightly on the planet, being kind to the environment, in our work? Does our work ennoble the spirit? Are we doing all that we can to clarify the relationship between spirituality and our work and life? Are we leaving a noble legacy? Is our work meaningful, just, and loving?

Inspirational leaders invest just as much time encouraging deeper spiritual and metaphysical awareness among parceners, introducing higher principles and the wisdom teachings of history as they do coaching them to greater efficiency and effectiveness. David Overton, the founder of the wildly successful Cheesecake Factory, of Calabassas Hills, California, asks waiters and waitresses to send "a little love" to customers, along with their delicious desserts. In his restaurants, "Stream of Life," murals featuring Sufi and other spiritual motifs decorate the ceilings. Overton uses astrology and numerology to optimize each new restaurant's "birth date." Overton, who studied comparative religion while at college, is very open about and committed to his Sufi beliefs, even wearing a winged Sufi heart ring on his hand, a symbol that is also discreetly in evidence on every menu. But the impact of these philosophies is much deeper. It helps provide the underpinnings of Overton's "philosophy of treating people." At an employee training meeting, Executive Vice-President Linda Candioty told an audience of thirty new employees, "The customers come in to eat and pay and leave, but they deserve something more. It might just be some love."

It is a mistake to think that weaving spiritual underpinnings into business organizations might lead to distraction or poor performance. On the contrary, it helps them to become more focused. The Cheesecake Factory averages among the highest sales per unit and the fastest growth rates in the industry, exports to many countries, has spun off a bakery sideline, and completed a successful IPO. Good servers earn over $40,000 a year, managers over $150,000 — and a new leased BMW.[40] When a spiritual compass guides organizations, it helps them to focus their strategy, and therefore enables leaders and parceners to agree on the rules for strategy implementation.

As the example of the Cheesecake Factory underscores, there is no need to trade off profit or performance for Values-centered Leadership™. We do not have to sacrifice bottom-line performance for a people-centered, caring, and sensitive leadership style that serves the parcener. On the contrary, we can have it all. The more we focus on serving our parceners, the more they will invent even better ways to enhance the bottom line. The one is the cause of the other — not a cost. The reverse is also true: the more we demand more and more with less and less, the more we will sap the spiritual energy of parceners and therefore damage organizational performance. The one is the obverse of the other.

A spiritual path can also lead to process improvements. In Zen Buddhism, there is a concept called the *gatha*, short verses that bring the energy of mindfulness to each act of daily life, including each task at work. All of our work activities can benefit from the practice of meditation or the use of *gathas*. Thich Nhat Hanh, the Vietnamese mystic, scholar, and activist Zen Buddhist monk, has written the following *gatha* that he uses when he is on the telephone:

Words can travel thousands of miles. May my words create mutual understanding and love. May they be beautiful as gems, as lovely as flowers.

What would happen if 1-800 call center employees invoked this *gatha* at the beginning of each day, or even each call? Would it lower stress, increase the desire to serve, building stronger and friendlier relationships with the public? Techniques like the *gatha* are both a spiritual practice — a way to ensure we serve others — and also an inspiring way to raise the bar on performance. Practices like the *gatha* are examples of how we can serve others better by inviting spirit to our work.

Practicing What We Preach

In 1896, Charles Sheldon, a Congregationalist minister from Topeka, Kansas, wrote a book called *In His Steps* (Uhrichsville, OH: Barbour Publishing), from which a burgeoning movement swept across the United States. It is known simply by the initials WWJD (What Would Jesus Do?). The book highlights the need to be of service to others, not just talk about it. Though set in a Christian context, the tale is equally relevant to people of any faith or philosophy.

The book tells the story of a vagrant denied practical compassion by the citizens of a devout and well-meaning community. One Sunday, after the congregation of the town church finishes singing hymns, he rises to speak to them. "It seems to me there's an awful lot of trouble in the world that somehow wouldn't exist if all the people who sing such songs went and lived them out. I suppose I just don't understand. But what would Jesus do? Is that what you mean by following His steps? It seems to me sometimes as if the people in the big churches had good clothes and nice houses to live in, and money to spend for luxuries, and could go away on summer vacations and all that, while the people outside the churches, thousands of them, I mean, die in tenements, and walk the streets for jobs, and never have a piano or a picture in the house, and grow up in misery and drunkenness and sin."

Later that morning, the vagrant dies in the minister's arms, shocking him into a reappraisal of what it means to follow in the steps of Christ. He issues a challenge to the congregation, asking them to live their lives from this day on by asking, "What would Jesus do?" before each and every decision in their lives. The rest of the book describes the major challenges faced by the editor of the newspaper, the local heiress, the manager of the railroad shops, and other citizens in the community as they struggle to honor their pledge to ask, "What would Jesus do?" before every important decision or action.

From this story has grown a movement: WWJD. Wrist-bands and T-shirts imprinted with the insignia WWJD are worn by hundreds of thousands of people. A subculture has grown around the theme, and a mini-industry has sprung up producing numerous books, CDs, and videos.

This story challenges us to ask ourselves whether we are simply demanding values-centered behavior from others, or whether we are modeling that behavior and therefore encouraging it in others.

Be the Change You Seek to Achieve

It is not good enough for us to sing the praises of our employees, describing them as our most important asset just before we fire five hundred of them. And hiring the outplacement firm to do the dirty work after the ax falls is not what Jesus would have done — or Jefferson or Martin Luther King — or my grandmother for that matter.

> **My father didn't tell me how to live; he lived, and let me watch him do it.**
>
> CLARENCE BUDDINTON KELLAND

The impact the WWJD story has had on so many people from all walks of life shows that people everywhere are searching for Inspirational Leaders who are prepared to accept their responsibility as role models, setting the standards of practice more than theory. To truly serve each other, we must be the kind of leader that inspires others through their deeds. To paraphrase Gandhi, the servant-leader must become the change they seek to achieve.

One day when Mahatma Gandhi was on a train pulling out of the station, a European reporter running alongside his compartment asked him, "Do you have a message I can take back to my people?" It was a day of silence for Gandhi, part of his regular practice, so he didn't reply. Instead, he scribbled a few words on a piece of paper, and then passed it to the journalist: "My life is my message."

We serve when we give. We serve best when we listen and then comply. This is greater than a mission statement.

THE INVITATION [41]

It doesn't interest me what you do for a living.
I want to know what you ache for,
and if you dare to dream of meeting your heart's longing.

It doesn't interest me how old you are.
I want to know if you will risk looking like a fool for love,
for your dreams, for the adventure of being alive.

It doesn't interest me what planets are squaring your moon.
I want to know if you have touched the center of your own sorrow,
if you have been opened by life's betrayals or have become shriveled and
closed from fear of further pain.

I want to know if you can sit with pain, mine or your own,
without moving to hide it or fade it or fix it.

I want to know if you can be with joy, mine or your own,
if you can dance with wildness and let the ecstasy fill you to the tips
of your fingers and toes
without cautioning us to be careful, be realistic, or to remember the
limitations of being human.

It doesn't interest me if the story you're telling me is true.
I want to know if you can disappoint another to be true to yourself;
if you can bear the accusation of betrayal and not betray your own soul.

I want to know if you can be faithless
and therefore be trustworthy.

I want to know if you can see beauty even when it is not pretty every day,
and if you can source your life from God's presence.

I want to know if you can live with failure, yours and mine,
and still stand on the edge of a lake and shout to the silver of the full moon,
"Yes"!

It doesn't interest me to know where you live
or how much money you have.
I want to know if you can get up after the night of grief and despair,
weary and bruised to the bone, and do what needs to be done
for the children.

It doesn't interest me who you are, how you came to be here.
I want to know if you will stand in the center of the fire
with me and not shrink back.

It doesn't interest me where or what or with whom you have studied.
I want to know what sustains you from the inside when all else falls away.

I want to know if you can be alone with yourself,
and if you truly like the company you keep in the empty moments.

BY ORIAH MOUNTAIN DREAMER

Step Six

Guiding the Contribution of Brilliance

After achieving pure clarity about their Destiny, defining and championing the Cause, reaffirming their commitment to their own Calling and coaching others to find and master theirs, aligning that Calling with the Cause, and asking the parcener "How may I serve you?," **the Inspirational Leader guides the parceners' contribution of brilliance**. The Inspirational Leader is therefore largely responsible for developing, nurturing, and building the *relationships* inside and outside the company. Parceners are responsible for everything else.

Another myth about great leaders is that they were all great strategists. Some of them were, but many were not. More important than anything else, they found brilliant people and inspired them. These brilliant parceners developed and implemented the strategies necessary to achieve the Cause. The Inspirational Leader is therefore largely responsible for developing, nurturing, and building the *relationships* inside and outside the company. Parceners are responsible for everything else.

Great organizations therefore have two distinct leadership activities: on the one hand, developing the Cause and fanning its flame — the role of the Inspirational Leader — and on the other hand, implementing the actions that make the Cause a reality — the role of the parcener. Inspirational Leaders understand that these two leadership tasks depend on the concept of disengagement. Disengagement is the leadership practice of deferring to those with a Calling, to those with the ability to implement. Inspirational Leaders inspire others sometimes by doing, but more often by *refraining from doing*. They inspire others by being Aquarian leaders, who tend to encourage parceners to fully utilize the power that lies within them.

In the symphony, the Inspirational Leader defines the Cause — the opus being played — and becomes its champion and guardian. The violinists implement the strategy that will make the Cause happen. The orchestra leader disengages from the implementation, focusing on the relationships among the team, and guiding their brilliance towards completion of the opus — the Cause.

In addition to the great myth that successful leaders always devise brilliant strategies is the accompanying myth that they must execute them brilliantly as well. This confines the roles of strategy formulation and implementation to the leader. This often results in a stifling, sycophantic culture where the leader functions as Helios, the sun god, and all other moons must remain in its shadow. When egos dominate so forcefully, there is not enough room for parceners to grow.

> **The queen bee does not take credit for the worker bees' doing their jobs effectively. She just does her job effectively, so that they can do theirs.**
>
> HENRY MINTZBERG

The real job of the leader is to make it easy for the parcener to develop and implement a brilliant strategy. The first violinist of a symphony will generally know more about playing the violin than the conductor will learn during his or her entire lifetime. However, the conductor is the keeper of the Cause — the opus he or she wishes to offer, how it is to be presented and the magic spell the symphony will weave over the audience. The orchestra leader has defined his or her own Destiny, followed a Calling, defined the Cause, and then aligned the Calling of the first violinist to the Cause, so that the violinist's gifts contribute to its achievement. Now it is time for the Inspirational Leader (the conductor) to offer to serve the violinist by providing any personal and professional support required, to help them grow and excel. This is the role of coach and guide. Now the Inspirational Leader is able to do one of the most important tasks — get out of the way. The Inspirational Leader empowers and enables the violinist to do what he or she knows how to do best — to play magnificently, as a virtuoso and as a member of an ensemble, in order to manifest the Cause. In other words, the leader guides the implementation of strategy. The leader's role is to guide the contribution of brilliance that lies waiting to be released from within the first violinist — like the contribution of brilliance that lies within us all. *Parceners are yearning for infusion, not intrusion.* The role of the conductor is to invite the violinist to release the music that lies within.

Inspiring People to Greatness

Leaders have long been urged to "concentrate on core competencies." Tom Peters and Bob Waterman told us that the successful organizations in search of excellence "stick to their knitting," focusing on what they do best, and *outsourcing* functions where they are weak.[42] A succession of management gurus has put their own spin onto this notion, but it all comes down to a simple general theory of core competencies: if we focus on what we do best, we will get better at it. The corollary is that organizations should stop doing those things that are areas of perceived weakness. The intent of this, of course, is to encourage corporate strategists to guide their organizations to higher performance, and corporate leaders have paid attention. The result has been a boom in the practice of subcontracting, outsourcing, and forging strategic alliances with others whose strengths complement our weaknesses.

But there is a paradox at work here. If it works so well with organizations, and if we buy the core competency idea so completely, why don't we apply the same principle to people? Guiding parceners to brilliance depends on our playing to their strengths, outsourcing, as it were, to them.

When I was the president of Manpower Limited, we had a franchisee called John Harold. To this day, I have not met his equal as a marketer. He was absolutely brilliant. But if he was the Leonardo da Vinci of sales and marketing, he was the Rube Goldberg of administration — he couldn't submit a form to save his life, let alone complete it accurately. I would visit his operations in a trance about his sales, rhapsodizing about his commercial achievements, and then I would say something like, "John, I haven't had a monthly sales summary report from you for eighteen months. Would you please start sending them?" He would assure me he would, then I would go home — and nothing would happen. My visits started to take on a similar pattern: ecstasy over his sales, despair about his forms. Once, after applauding another record-breaking sales performance that set a stratospheric standard for the rest of the company to follow, I gamely asked him if he would consider sending me a monthly summary once a quarter. He agreed (but nothing happened!).

I was the CEO and I was supposed to be the teacher and coach, but I began to realize it was John Harold who was giving the lessons. Finally, he reached me and I got it. I went down to his office one day and I said, "John, whenever I visit you, I always compliment you on your brilliant sales performance and then I complain about your sales summaries. I am here to promise you that the last time I did this was the last time I will ever do so. I have hired someone on my payroll to complete your monthly summaries. I will never nag you again about your sales summaries. Now, how can I help you with your sales? How can I serve you?" We never looked back.

Whatever gave me the idea that I could turn one of the finest marketers I had ever met in my entire life into — at best — a mediocre form-filler? Why would I want to? Why was I so arrogant? Why would I try to reduce him to a corporate, multi-competencied clone? Here was a one-of-a-kind genius, and I was about to squander his gifts and extinguish the flames of his inspiration. Strategy implementation is not about getting everyone to do something the same way. It is about playing to their strengths, teasing greatness from them by honoring their gifts, and making it as easy as possible for them to be brilliant at what they do — guiding the brilliance of their contribution. Dilberts are intimidated into doing everything the same way, and thus perform in the margins; da Vincis do everything in a way that plays to their strengths, and thus perform brilliantly. Sameness and conformity are easier to manage, but their price is mediocrity and demotivation. On the other hand, guiding brilliance is like herding cats, but a gift to the soul — inspiration.

> **Things don't change. You change your way of looking, that's all.**
>
> CARLOS CASTANEDA

Marcel Proust said, "The real voyage of discovery comes not in seeking new landscapes but in having new eyes." If we wish to inspire others, we will need to work on their strengths instead of carping about their weaknesses. We need to know that the principle of focusing on our core competencies is as sound for individuals as it is for organizations. This is a key to illuminating people, nourishing their souls and inspiring them to greatness.

Brilliance and the Balance-Point

The two Chinese characters that make up the word *busy* are the symbols for "heart" and "death." In guiding the brilliance of parceners, we need to restore some semblance of balance to their lives. As the pace of work life spirals faster and faster, we will not be able to expect brilliance from harried parceners. It is unfair and illogical. The Inspirational Leader works hard to remove rather than add clutter to parceners' lives.

Powered by indefatigable confidence, humans have spent centuries attempting to roll back the natural world, to disturb the natural balance-point. We have striven to tame nature, often successfully, in a million different ways. But the laws of nature are immutable and will only yield temporarily to humans. Everything seeks to find its balance-point, and in the end, everything does.

Where I live, the stone walls of farms built one hundred years ago are barely visible today beneath the tangles of brambles and accumulating earth. An abandoned hydro-electric dam that once powered mills, hotels, and homes has now fallen into disrepair as the river restores the site to its original state with humbling inevitableness. We used to be a thriving community with a railroad station and three hotels. Now we are a quiet hamlet of seventy-two people.

The changes we impose on nature are illusory, because the underlying Laws remain active and in force, even when they are not apparent. In the end, the Natural Laws always prevail. Meanwhile, if we challenge them, the energy of those Laws will oppose us. The overarching principle behind the Laws of Nature is the need to seek a balance-point — for every action there is a corresponding and opposing action. This *yin* and *yang* of Nature is the Law of Life.

These same Natural Laws apply in our own lives and especially in our relationships. Negative energy (emotions, ideas, actions, and communications) attracts similar energy. If we seek paths that attempt to disturb the balance in our lives, the immutable Laws of Nature work to return our lives to their original balance-points. The rate of pain, suffering, and stress we experience will tend to be matched by the degree to which we stray from this balance-point. Though the matching energy may not always occur in the same time frame, it will eventually return to the balance-point. This is as inevitable as the erosion of the stone walls of the farm or the river's will to submerge the abandoned hydro-electric dam.

Just as surely, acts of loving-kindness will attract similar forces. The difference between negative and positive energy is that the balance-point is a place of perfect energy. The Natural Laws of the Universe are loving laws. Introducing negative energy that disturbs this balance-point attracts a correcting, negative force. Positive energy, that is, energy that respects the balance-point, on the other hand, merely reinforces the equilibrium of the Natural Laws and needs no correcting energy field.

This matches the Buddha's teachings of the Four Noble Truths: (1) Life is suffering; (2) All suffering is caused by ignorance of the nature of reality and the craving, attachment, and grasping that result from such ignorance;

(3) Suffering can be ended by overcoming ignorance and attachment; (4) The path to the suppression of suffering is the Noble Eightfold Path, which consists of right views, right intention, right speech, right action, right livelihood, right effort, right-mindedness, and right contemplation. These eight are usually divided into three categories that form the cornerstone of Buddhist faith: morality, wisdom, and s*amadhi,* or concentration.

And so we come full circle. The secret to achieving the balance-point in our lives — essential for brilliant achievement — is to respect the Natural Laws of the Universe. If we complain about the lack of balance in our lives while creating the very negative energy that creates the imbalance, we should not be surprised. We can't have it both ways; the Natural Laws will not allow it. When we push against the balance-points of life — by acquiring more, by using more than our share of resources, by seeking to dominate or control markets, customers, employees, family and friends, by destroying competitors, by pushing people beyond their limits — we set up an inevitable cycle of reciprocal negative energy.

In a university commencement address several years ago, Brian Dyson, CEO of Coca-Cola Enterprises, spoke of the relationship between work and one's other commitments: "Imagine life as a game in which you are juggling some five balls in the air. You name them — work, family, health, friends, and spirit — and you're keeping all of these in the air. You will soon understand that work is a rubber ball. If you drop it, it will bounce back. But the other four balls — family, health, friends, and spirit — are made of glass. If you drop one of these, they will be irrevocably scuffed, marked, nicked, damaged, or even shattered. They will never be the same. You must understand that and strive for balance in your life."

Balance in our lives is achieved by finding our balance-point, not by searching endlessly for more and more with less and less.

Leadership Is Not a Drive-Through Experience

Life is not a journey; it is a collection of moments. We are not destined to follow or create a path to somewhere. This is a typically modern, narcissistic notion. We are destined to live each moment with passion, preferably in the service of others. That is a definition of joy. Guiding the brilliance of parceners is achieved by being present with them, by being in the moment, and paying attention. We need to enjoy the journey together just as much as the arrival at a destination.

On a recent trip, I looked out of the window as the plane touched down in Denver, and I knew the flight was so late that I would miss my shuttle to Vail. I reflected on how I might turn this inconvenience into fun.

My imagination considered out-of-the-box alternatives. I have a secret: I am a Mustang-aholic — I rent Mustang convertibles whenever I can in exotic locales like the Florida Everglades or the California coastline. I sensed that my current inconvenience could be an opportunity for a Mustang lover. So I rented a silver ragtop and set about floating up the mountains with the top down, breathing in the essence of pine and leaving my road-warrior cares behind me. Eagerly I set out on the 118-mile drive, through the foothills, past defunct gold and silver mines, bustling ski areas, bighorn sheep, white-tailed deer, waterfalls, big sky, and mountain magic.

> **Fun is when you enjoy what you are doing; work is when you'd rather be doing something else.**
>
> ART BUCK

I could handle this — a two-hour treat for the spirit. The engine roared to life and I lowered the top — I was on my way, heading west on the I70.

I soon realized this would not be a soporific snooze. Yes, the road is beautiful — but BUSY! The entire world population of Mack Truckers, it seemed, was heading to Vail for a convention. Thirty-wheelers towered around me everywhere, thundering alongside like a huge herd of Belgian horses next to my pony — no margin for error. Also the State of Colorado had decided to lavish its entire energy that evening on the I70, undertaking a dizzying array of road works and construction. Road-ragers joined the thunderous herd careening west, all trying to clip a second or two from their journey, cutting me off, pushing in front, and then hitting the brakes. A dawdling Magic Wagon wandered into the passing lane, loaded with two kayaks, a Coleman's warehouse of camping gear (there must have been a partridge in a pear tree somewhere in there, too), and created a trail of road-rage a mile long. This wasn't fun — this was hard, dirty work — like horseback riding in the middle of a buffalo stampede.

Looking around, I saw people talking on their cell phones, truckers chasing their bonuses, cab-drivers dashing to their destinations so they could squeeze in another fare, and highway contractors racing against performance deadlines. Entering a two-mile tunnel, I closed my nose, hoping I could hold my breath until the tunnel exit, but I had to relent, inhaling through an impromptu mask I fashioned from my shirtsleeve. Then it started to rain — so much for the convertible idea. Just as well perhaps — the ninety-degree heat at the airport plunged quickly to a chilly fifty degrees in the mountains.

I smiled to myself as it occurred to me that this is a metaphor for our lives at work. I want to be a human being, not a human doing. I want to be, not do. I want to smell the mountain air as I glide through the granite passes and ravines in a car that is ideal for this experience. I yearn to drink in the awesome scenery, discover the subtle camouflages of nature, and submit myself to the majesty of the high country. I want to savor life when I work and when I play. But often I dare not participate in this experience of life, because getting there will require my full concentration if I am not to succumb to the hazards around me. I can't do both — there is no balance here. I must forgo the experience in favor of the process; it's just like work. If I am not vigilant, I will become the prisoner of process instead of a participant in the experience.

How much of our time is spent on the means rather than the ends — the rules and policies, the structures (strategic plans, budgets, proposals, compensation programs, agendas, etc.) and the rituals (meetings, voice mail, e-mail, performance appraisals, agendas, and politics)?

Leadership is not so much about technique and methods as it is about opening the heart. Leadership is about inspiration — of oneself and of others. Great leadership is about human experiences, not processes. Leadership is not a formula or a program. It is a human activity, which comes from the heart and considers the hearts of others. It is an attitude, not a routine. Leadership is not a drive-through experience.

More than anything else today, parceners believe they are part of "a system," a process, that lacks heart. If there is one thing a leader can do to connect with parceners at a human — or more precisely, a spiritual — level, it is to become engaged with them fully, to share experiences and emotions, and to set aside the processes of leadership we have learned by rote.

Leadership is a simple idea — it is an act of love and balance. Guiding the brilliance of parceners requires Inspirational Leaders to be in the moment with them — sharing, inspiring, while serving them and getting out of their way, disengaging — not doing.

"How Do We Get Them to Change?"

Guiding the contribution of brilliance of others requires us to relate with them at levels beyond the day-to-day, beyond the mundane with which we have become comfortable, beyond the data and the performance ratios, beyond the material and the physical. It requires us to relate with each other in a values-centered, metaphysical, spiritual way. This requires us to reframe our approach to relationships and communications, by being brave and authentic, opening our hearts, and maintaining a state of grace. In much of my work, I am told that this is simply too much to expect people to accomplish all at once. It is too big a leap; the change is too dramatic. Everyone knows that we need to change, but we need to do so in bite-sized chunks.

The question that I am most frequently asked in my work is, "How do we get *them* to change?" There is often a sense in people's minds that the people who really need to hear this message of change are not in the audience. This, of course, is a classic case of projection. When we say that we really understand truth-telling, promise-keeping, integrity, trust, respect, values, and spirit and that it is the other people who don't "get it," our shadow is really saying "*I* don't yet get it." When we point a finger at someone else, three fingers point back at ourselves. This is another example of projection.

This is especially true when we consider the concept of critical mass reviewed in chapter 2. There is a growing sense that more and more people are indeed "getting it," and that it has now become more important that we signal to others that *we* now get it, too.

Of course this is not the easiest thing in the world to do, and so the second most frequently asked question that I hear in my work is, "How do I actually achieve this transformation?" There are four important attitudes that are essential for practicing Inspirational Leadership®. They are:

1. Courage
2. Authenticity
3. Love
4. Grace

Courage

Much of the work of the Inspirational Leader is modeling behavior for others. We all know that we should love one another, and most of us know how to, we just need someone we respect to actually say the words in practice, in a real world, work-a-day situation. Until then, these concepts remain ideals, little more than nice theories better suited to a different kind of world than the one most of us believe we live in. It's like karaoke singing for most people — if you go first, I'll follow you, but don't ask me to start!

Being an Inspirational Leader takes courage. Without courage we are not able to take even the first steps because they contain so much perceived risk. When we tell people at work that we love them, we don't want them to think that we just flew in from a commune in California. Our perception of this risk is, of course, framed by our egos. We are afraid of how we will be judged and that our personalities might be diminished by the criticism of others. The soul understands the need and the desire to take the appropriate action to change culture and actions at work, but the ego stands in the way.

A ship in harbour is safe, but that is not what ships are built for.

WILLIAM SHEDD

Until we listen to our inner voices, to our souls, inviting our egos to take a secondary role, courage will not be present, but when we do, courage will emerge and give us the one thing that we lack — will. It is the will to make change that starts the process; it is the will that invests fire into our passion, impelling us to become the instruments of change.

Courage gives us the will to do what is necessary to make change, to rise above the intimidation that our personalities experience from the personalities of others.

Authenticity

When we acquire courage, we become authentic. It is not until we become brave enough that we have the courage to be real. Being real is not about hiding our truth, about hiding our emotions, and vulnerabilities. On the contrary, it is about revealing them. It is about showing our fears to each other and speaking our truth. It is about aligning our hearts and our mouths and our minds. When we are authentic, we say, and do, what we mean.

As long as we believe that everyone else should tell truth, but don't actually do it ourselves, we are being inauthentic. When we are inauthentic in this way, we are hypocritical. When we say that everyone should be truthful and then fail to be so ourselves, we are not only being inauthentic, but even worse, we are inauthentic leaders. This does two things: firstly, it sends a signal to parceners that we are incongruent, that our walk doesn't match our talk, and, secondly, it gives parceners permission to behave the same way as the leader — inauthentically.

Parceners love authentic leaders. Authenticity, as much as anything, generates love in the hearts of others. When we think of those people in our lives whom we have loved dearly and deeply, the common thread that runs through them all is their shining authenticity. We call people like these "straight arrows," "true blue," high-integrity people.

Doug Upchurch faced some extreme personal challenges when he joined the Information Technology Training Association:

Shortly after I joined the association, I discovered some legal and financial issues that I was unaware I would have to deal with. During the first few days, I was reviewing some reports, and uncovered what appeared to be significant financial discrepancies. I had to deal with this issue, which was complicated by the fact that my predecessor was a very dear friend of mine. In addition to this, his wife was doing meeting and conference planning work with us. Tragically, on the eve of our annual national conference, he chose to take his life.

We were all in a state of disbelief, and I was twenty-seven! We take a week off after all conferences anyway, so this provided time with our loved ones to deal with it, too. We also had a memorial at the conference, which we held in his honor at the golf course — one of his favorite places. During the conference, our members and board members were on hand to help and support each other.

Afterwards, a number of emotional issues emerged. At our staff meetings, we kept our focus on *how* is everybody doing? rather than *what* is everyone doing? We asked ourselves if we could have done anything differently. Has anyone talked to the late founding executive director's wife? Has anyone gone to the gravesite? Every day, we got calls asking for him, and we'd have to share the news with the callers. It was a very difficult process.

I had come on board with this organization with the intent to take it to the next level. I had to tell the president and treasurer and my staff (his former employees) about the financial discrepancies and my friend's passing. We didn't know if the association would survive financially. I found my staff and myself in a grieving process over the loss of our friend, who, to our staff and me, was an industry hero.

About three weeks later, I woke up one night crying and screaming with the pain of it all. I was rattled, and I was thinking to myself, "I

don't want to become like that." I thought he'd lost sight of his purpose, his family, and his friends. I didn't want that to happen to me.
He had died the first week of June, and I said I'd never let any employee
who worked for me let work become more important than their
personal life.

Earlier in my career, I was paying more attention to duties and functions than to people. As soon as I shifted my thinking and started to
pay greater attention to people, our effectiveness took off. It was my
desire that we would be an association committed to people, and my
staff knew that I would support them in any way whenever they needed
to take care of issues in their personal lives — even if it meant missing
deadlines or delaying projects. I know I will never let people lose sight
of what matters most, and what matters most is the *people* — employees, customers, and suppliers.

Those are the words of an authentic leader, deep in the messy realities of
life, dealing with emotions and difficult issues on a personal basis, earning
the love and affection of parceners and others who know him. Doug is an
Inspirational Leader.

Love

As Doug Upchurch's story illustrates, authenticity and genuineness lead to
love. It is very difficult not to fall in love with authentic
people. They are consistent, dependable, transparent,
steady, loyal, and reliable. Their messages are concor-
dant, their beliefs unwavering, and their opinions valued. Doug defines his role as an Inspirational Leader
this way: "I see myself as a steward and I see myself as
a leader. I am a trustee — the care of parceners' souls
while they are here is my job. I need to care as much
about their well-being spiritually and emotionally as I do about them pro-
fessionally. I am not just checking tasks. I am also checking on how people
are doing. Worrying about what I think should not be their guiding force."

Aquarian leader archetypes not only attract love as a result of their
authenticity, they project love, too. Their courage, which leads to their authenticity, causes them to transmit and communicate love. Great servant leaders,

> **Wherever there is a human being, there is an opportunity for kindness.**
>
> SENECA

some of the greatest Aquarian leaders in history, Gandhi, Jefferson, Nelson Mandela, Mother Teresa, Buddha — all shared these characteristics: courage, authenticity, and love. They loved and were loved.

To him who is in fear everything rustles.

SOPHOCLES

At the other end of the continuum from love, there exists a shadow called fear. The shadow of fear will only surrender to light. It is the intense light of love, when shone directly into the eyes of fear that causes it to shrink and fade. Thus love reinforces our courage and enables us to be more consistently authentic.

We are not altogether comfortable with this notion in our Western culture. There are ninety-six words for love in the Sanskrit-based languages, eighty in Persian, three in Greek — but only one in English. The Anglo-Saxon heritage rests uneasily when it comes to expressing our feelings, but we all want to hear the same message — that we are loved. We struggle with feelings of awkwardness when we attempt to express our love for our colleagues, leaders, parceners, customers, and suppliers, yet they all crave to be loved just as much as we do. It takes courage to say what we really feel — that we love the people we work with when this is so. Courage also enables us to become more authentic, and therefore more lovable. Love animates the relationship between the Inspirational Leader and the parcener. It is *the* reason why parceners and leaders maintain a continuing and growing relationship.

Wisdom tells me I am nothing; love tells me I am everything. Between the two, my life flows.

AN INDIAN MASTER

Grace

It takes courage to be authentic, but when we are, our authenticity generates love — within the hearts of others and our own. The love experienced by Inspirational Leaders and their parceners creates a state of grace. To love and to be loved is to experience grace. Inspired organizations contain substantial measures of all four characteristics — courage, authenticity, love, and grace.

I often use the following metaphor to illustrate how important it is for us to be in the moment and to practice the behavior we wish to see in others. Imagine that you are in Vietnam in a foxhole during the Vietnam war with one other soldier. All around you is a living hell — bombs are dropping, napalm is scorching the earth, explosions and screams surround you, and you are terrified. There is very little you can do about all this. This external world is not controlled by you, but by "them." The one thing you do have control over is the quality of the relationship between you and the other soldier, the other soul with whom you are sharing this experience, this human being beside you with whom you share your foxhole. If you ensure that you are both in a state of grace at all times, you will win, no matter what happens to your physical form. If you die, you will be in a state of grace together, up to and including your final moments. If you live, you will be in a state of grace together, too. Either way, you will create a spiritual energy that will transcend the things over which it seems you have little control. We all have the same choices at work. We can invest our energy in demanding that others change, or we can put the same energy into maintaining a state of grace with our colleagues, customers, and suppliers at all times, influencing their behavior through our own actions.

When people ask me, "How do we get *them* to change?" or suggest, "*They* don't get it," I ask them first to ask themselves this question, "Am I fully present and inviting my full potential of courage, authenticity, love, and grace to my work and life?"

When we can say that we are, then we will be perfect and entitled to advise others. Until then, Inspirational Leaders keep moving to the edges of their comfort zones, becoming more courageous, being more authentic and loving, and being loved and striving to be in a state of grace. This inspires parceners and helps them to display and contribute their brilliance.

Escape [43]

When we get out of the glass bottles of our ego,
And we escape like squirrels turning in the cages of our personality
and get into the forests again,
we shall shiver with cold and fright
but things will happen to us
so that we don't know ourselves.

Cool, unlying life will rush in,
and passion will make our bodies taught with power,
we shall stamp our feet with new power
and old things will fall down,
we shall laugh, and institutions will curl up like burnt paper.

D.H. LAWRENCE

Step Seven

Magic Ingredient X:
Creating the Environment to Inspire

Finally, after achieving pure clarity about one's Destiny, defining and championing the Cause, reaffirming their commitment to their own Calling and coaching others to find and master theirs, aligning the Calling with the Cause, asking the parcener, "How may I serve you?" and guiding the parceners' contribution of brilliance, the Inspirational Leader creates the environment that encourages parceners to inspire the leader. All leaders need to be inspired, and their followers are a vital source of inspiration.

Inspirational Leadership® is leadership that comes from the heart and soul. Its applicability as a leadership approach is not limited to corporations, but is equally relevant in families, churches, governments, health care, law enforcement agencies, educational organizations and communities — anywhere where groups of people combine to advance the purpose of the human spirit. We are all leaders, and our purpose is to inspire others.

Another popular myth about leadership is that leaders possess bottomless reservoirs of energy and resilience, and, like the Energizer bunny, their batteries will outlast those of everyone else. Many leaders act out this myth, pretending that they are invulnerable and capable of regenerating themselves without any input from others.

We all know, whether we admit it or not, that leaders need to be inspired just like anyone else, because they are humans. The most important source of this inspiration is the people whom leaders lead and inspire. But leaders cannot demand inspiration from parceners; they must create the environment that encourages such inspiration. I call this "Magic Ingredient X" because it is a missing component in almost all leadership thinking. There is no one right way to achieve this, but there are a number of ways that have been tested over time. One is to build the spiritual energy of the team, and this is one of the Inspirational Leader's most important roles. Parceners, in turn, will reward the Inspirational Leader with inspiration.

Enhancing the SQ of Teams

All teams encounter difficulties — life is both a mystery and a puzzle. The soul views these events with equanimity, but the personality is less forgiving. Events do not always unfold as our egos would wish, and this may cause us to gossip, vent, and complain about things, very often about each other. In a team that has become a Sanctuary, where we have raised our spiritual awareness, these ego-based forms of communication often give way to a more loving style of communication. We each have choices for communicating and resolving our frustrations.

Have you ever noticed how some people steal power from a team? Energy vampires are present in many teams, draining the collective energy from them and causing a shift from being inspired to tired. The soul wilts in these conditions, and the energy barometer plummets.

Think about the people you work with, the members of teams to which you belong — what is their Spiritual Quotient (SQ)? Think of SQ as a casual litmus test that you might apply to people whom you do not know well. When you think about these people, where do they range on a scale of 0 to 10, with zero being very low and ten being very high? Is this person quite spiritually aware, perhaps having an SQ of, say, 7, or are they drawing spiritual energy from the team, having an SQ of, say, 2? Are they spiritually awakened, or do they remain far from embarking fully on a spiritual path? This is not meant to be a prescriptive formula, nor is it intended to be judgmental, but rather to make us aware of what we are looking for in teams. It is important for us to always ask the question so that we remain aware of each other's spiritual development, choosing where we can to contribute to the spiritual energy of a team, and to work with people who are on the same journey as ourselves, even if we may be on different roads and at different stages. We are interested in ensuring that spirit and values are showing up on a person's radar and that they are growing as spiritual beings. As leaders and parceners, we are interested in knowing whether others are depositing or withdrawing spiritual energy, thus enhancing or depleting the collective SQ of the team.

All team members, including leaders, have a critical responsibility: to contribute power to the group and to build the SQ of the entire team. The question we each need to ask is, "Will everyone else be inspired as a result of what I am about to say?" If we cannot answer "yes," we should pause, because it is the responsibility of every team member to inspire all of the others, *all of the time* — even when it seems that our will to do so is depleted. Although there is a great deal of academic research and theory about this subject, the bare essential is that all our exchanges within teams must energize each other — in every direction and in every communication within the team. It is not someone else's responsibility — it is *our* responsibility.

This also raises the question, "Who is the leader?" Surely everyone, at some point or another, must assume a leadership responsibility? This is what members of great teams do all the time, whether they are medical teams, volunteer organizations, symphonies, or religious congregations. In my earlier book, *The Way of the Tiger*, Moose, the wise tiger, teaches values to his community and defines this shared responsibility for leadership in his inimitable way: *Moose's Law of Leadership: In a team of 100 people, there are 100 leaders.*[44] Leadership is not an activity for "them," nor is it limited to the person at "the top." It is the responsibility of every human who is present on this planet, regardless of age, function, race, material status, or any other condition. We are spiritual beings enjoying a human experience, and we are all leaders. We need to ask, all the time, "Am I behaving in a way that affirms not just the personalities of everyone in the team, but their souls, too?" In other words, are we practicing Inspirational Leadership®? Are we inspiring each other in every communication and working positively without exceptions?

> **In saying what I have in mind, will I really improve on the silence?**
>
> ROBERT K. GREENLEAF

The Art of Followership

We hear a great deal about leadership and how leaders should lead, but we hear much less about followership: how parceners can best serve each other, their leader, and their community. In building relationships, the roles of leader and parcener are part of a hologram; they are all part of the same relationship, just seen from different perspectives.

A great speech, for example, can be made or broken by the quality of the introduction — the way the speaker is "set up." Similarly, leadership often depends on the quality of the followership. The Inspirational Leader teaches parceners how to follow, and part of the art of followership is knowing when and how to lead. Everyone leads at some time. Siblings take turns leading; parents alternate between themselves and their children in leading and following. Spouses and partners practice leadership and followership responsibilities at different times; so do customers and suppliers, senior and junior team members, members of a cast, a band or a sports team — all juggle the responsibilities of leading and following as appropriate. The more they know about the dynamics of leadership and followership, the more effective the relationships will be. The Aquarian leader shares power in this way, recognizing the need to maximize material and spiritual power in both leader and parceners.

Parceners contribute greatly to the leadership process by:

- Promoting, protecting and remaining supportive to the Cause
- Being passionate about their Calling
- Telling the truth and keeping promises to each other and the leader (and everyone else)
- Inspiring each other and the leader
- Being open and willing to learn and change
- Teaching each other and learning together
- Always remaining alert to potential new team members and bringing them onto the team
- Being adaptable and capable of leading when appropriate
- Contributing to the team energy
- Augmenting the spiritual intensity of the team (SQ)

One of the most important roles of parceners is to give emotional and spiritual support to Inspirational Leaders — all the time, but especially in moments of stress, crisis, or loneliness. Aquarian leaders are frequently subject to frailties, just like the rest of us, because, just like the rest of us, they are human. Incredible leader though he was, Martin Luther King, Jr., had his shadow side, too. He was frequently plagued with doubts about what to do next in the civil liberties movement. Over many years, the FBI wiretapped King's home and office, putting bugs into his hotel rooms, where they recorded his numerous sexual liaisons. He suffered from depression and despair. Although he enjoyed the loyalty of many, he also endured constant opposition from many of his colleagues.[45] For all this, he was one of the greatest leaders in our century, and this could not have happened without the strong support of those who loved and followed him and were passionate about his Cause.

In essentials Unity, in non-essentials Freedom, in all things Charity.

ST. AUGUSTINE

Affirmation for a Parcener

Today I Will:

- Not judge
- Share
- Live only in the present
- Tell the truth
- Say sorry

- Forgive
- Commit to new learning
- Listen
- Serve
- Inspire

Everybody on earth knowing
That beauty is beautiful
Makes ugliness.

Everybody knowing
That goodness is good
Makes wickedness.

For being and nonbeing
Arise together;
Hard and easy
Complete each other;
Long and short
Shape each other
High and low
Depend on each other;
Note and voice
Make the music together;
Before and after
Follow each other.

That's why the wise soul
Does without doing,
Teaches without talking.

The things of this world
Exist, they are;
You can't refuse them.

To bear and not to own;
To act and not lay claim;
To do the work and let it go:
For just letting it go
Is what makes it stay.

TAO TE CHING[46]

Talk to My Yin

For much of my life, I have been plagued with a paradox. On the one hand, I seek to live (that is, think, act, and communicate), with love, compassion, kindness, truth, and grace. On the other hand, I often find myself thinking, acting, and communicating with anger, hostility, or judgment. I have graduated from many of the conventional therapies in my search for understanding of this personal idiosyncrasy, and while I sense I am getting better, I still detect the presence of a trickster, the wily character of Native American folklore, lurking somewhere in my inner space. This trickster confounds my good intentions from time to time.

When we match the energy of those with whom we communicate, we give away our power to them. The dynamics would be different if we reacted with balancing energy. The exquisite rhythms of life are dependent on perfect balance — *yin* and *yang,* the warp and woof of life — light and dark, beautiful and ugly, loving and fearsome, accepting and judgmental, masculine and feminine. Life cannot exist and unfold without this balance. Thus we need both, even though *yang* energy may frustrate or disappoint us from time to time. It helps to view *yang* energy as a great teacher, offering lessons about the issues in our lives that we need to address. Buddha said that the purpose of our enemies is for us to learn from them. When presented with *yang* energy, we have choices — we can invite the trickster to dance, or ask the question, "What am I being asked to learn by this *yang* energy?"

The wise learn many things from their enemies.

ARISTOPHANES

I received an understanding of my uncomfortable paradox following a recent meditation. Like most of us, my behavior falls into two types — *yang*: assertive, decisive, focused, and competitive, and *yin*: loving, graceful, compassionate, kind, and truthful. A search of my relationship patterns reveals that some people generate more *yang* energy, causing me to engage more of my own *yang* energy. Others generate more of their *yin* energy, which arouses more of the *yin* energy within me. Although we are all a combination of *yin* and *yang* energies, I find certain people tend to trigger more *yang* reactions and responses in me, while others gently coax more *yin* behavior from me.

My conscious thought is influenced by my shadow, that unconscious part of me that contains my wishes, memories, fears, feelings, and ideas. My shadow is too easily goaded into a *yang* response by people who address me with *yang* energy, and my *yin* energy is easily and willingly seduced when it is addressed by *yin* energy. It is as if visitors who show up at my door can choose either one of two pals with whom to dance — *yin* or *yang*. If the visitor asks for *yang*, watch out, because that's whom they will get; and if they ask for *yin*, a gentle soul will emerge as their partner. They both reside in the same house, and neither of them has any prior commitments on their dance card.

> **Love cures people — both the ones who give it and the ones who receive it.**
>
> DR. KARL MENNINGER

All this presents another paradox. Though it may appear to some that *yin* conveys positive energy and *yang* conveys negative, in fact, they each convey both and they each convey neither. It is our reaction that alters the energy. Therefore, when communicating, our role is to balance the energy we receive. When we receive *yang* energy, we need to respond with an appropriate blend of *yang* **and** *yin*, bringing balance to the communication, thus making it whole, and creating a relationship infused with spirit. Before I respond to powerful *yang* energy, I pause, reflect and then restrain the trickster who is itching to be unleashed, and instead offer a *yin* response, thus balancing the dialogue. When I remember, it works like a charm!

When we learn to invite the balance of *yin* and *yang*, we are able to control communications by moderating our responses. This is inspiring for the parceners and thus invites inspiring behavior from them. For example, if we respond to aggression with hot energy, it will attract even hotter energy. If we respond with calm energy, it will cool down the responding hot energy and the ensuing dialogue. I have found, too, that I can choose to associate with *yin* people or with *yang*. More than anything else, I now know this: if I wish to inspire others, even those who bring me too much *yang* energy, it is wise to respond to them with *yin* energy nevertheless. Our world culture favors *yang* communications and invites the *yang* trickster within us all to dance. We need to shift the energy from *yang* to *yin* in order to create mutual inspiration.

Knowing this, I have another approach available to me: I can invite everyone with whom I interact to address my *yin*. Failure to do so risks offering a dance invitation to the trickster who lives within. This does not entitle me to hand over the responsibility for my communications and relationships to third parties. It simply means that you and I are always partners, seeking to achieve a spiritual connection, and in doing so, we must teach each other how to communicate effectively. The secret to building inspired relationships and being an Inspirational Leader in a *yang* world is to balance our energy from *yang* to *yin* whenever possible in our relationships and in our responses.

Beyond Therapy: Accepting Personal Responsibility in Teams

For forty years, Western societies have been swept along in a sea of assorted therapies that have exhorted us to love ourselves first before we can love others, and to respect our inner children and many other characters, demons, and specters. It is time to move beyond self-centered approaches towards attitudes that focus on serving others. We do not have a divine right to rationalize our dysfunctional behavior by referring to our abusive upbringing, broken family heritage, and endless other wounds. This is simply self-indulgent activity that drains power from others. It is hard to imagine Mother Teresa or Martin Luther King emotionally hijacking a meeting by unburdening the emotional baggage of their early life. It is time to unlink ourselves from this adolescent thinking, assume our leadership responsibilities, and wean ourselves from emotional co-dependency within teams. The Inspirational Leader knows that it is more therapeutic to fulfill dreams than to analyze them.

There is simply no excuse for displaying dysfunctional behavior at work — ranting, rage, anger, violence, rudeness, shouting, heated arguments, cursing, storming out of meetings, hanging up the phone on someone, throwing things, and so on. Yet, I hear about behavior of this kind all the time in my work — among grown-up adults! There is much we can do about this sort of behavior, including telling each other the truth about our feelings, offering and seeking professional advice, maintaining a daily state of grace with each other, loving each other, making a promise to heal each other, accepting responsibility for the pain our behavior causes, and inviting the friendship and support of our colleagues. What is not acceptable is to continue to drain energy from the team and destroy the possibility of building one that is inspired. We must do our inner work, accept responsibility for our behavior, and recognize that there is only one reason why teams become dysfunctional — it is because *we* (that usually means *I*) feed dysfunctional behavior into it.

Doug Upchurch, former Executive Director of the Information Training Association, says, "My heart-cry in leadership is that if we are to effectively lead employees, we need to support their personal healing as much as their professional growth."

Healing is a necessary transition for all of us, but not a permanent way station. We must honor each other's needs to heal with patience, understanding, and compassion. Wounds that took time to accumulate will also take time to heal. Though we all need to visit a place of healing to repair our inherited wounds, we cannot park there forever. After overcoming the denial and repression of our past injuries, we must undertake the work of completion, closing the past and beginning our true Destiny: being a loving human. After we have concluded our necessary therapies, we must begin the greatest therapy of all, which is to serve others. In doing so, we will be served, healed, and therefore inspired. This is the special gift of the Inspirational Leader and the enlightened parcener.

The dynamics of teams show that we need to mature and move on. As we sit in teams nursing our wounds — what medical intuitive, Caroline Myss, calls "woundology" behavior — we drain power from each other, build resentment among members, and weaken the team.[47] As a result, we lower the SQ by leaching toxins into team chemistry, goading each other's egos, and creating dysfunctional battles among them. If we shift our energy from victim behavior to inspiring behavior, we will dramatically change the energy and the SQ of the entire team. This is one of the hallmarks of Inspirational Leadership®. If we raise the SQ of others on the team, even when it is the last thing in the world we are motivated to do at that time, it will lift their souls, and they in turn will respond by lifting ours. If we need to be healed, we can start by healing others, even when our own needs are greater. Others will be inspired to heal us in response. In other words, we get what we give.

When we choose to serve, we inspire. Remember that the meaning of inspire is to breathe "the breath of God." First, we inspire each other. Then we will *conspire* — which means to breathe together — from *con* "with" and *spirare* "to breathe." The resulting healing of our wounds is the gift that teams bestow on members who serve. We are not put on this planet just to follow our bliss — we are here to create bliss — and that is how we follow our bliss.

When leaders and parceners see these transformations taking place, they become inspired. Watching a team grow, heal, and learn to inspire each other is a marvel for a leader. Each of us can give light — if we stay bright. Parceners so inspired experience a mystical urge to inspire others — including the leader. They are joyful, and joyful people cannot resist sharing their joy.

Creating an Environment That Inspires Others to Inspire

We encourage violence when we practice violence. The dysfunctional actions we observe in others are often the response of their unconscious self to our conscious behavior. When our leadership patterns are based on Arian warrior-leader archetypes, driven solely by selfish motives which we call budgets, targets, quotas, performance criteria, goals, strategies, plans, and so on, we elicit selfish behavior in response. Violence and love are at opposite ends of a continuum, with selfishness at one end and service at the other. *What we give is what we get.* This is one of the foundations of Inspirational Leadership®.

Many leaders focus so much of their time on *their own* needs — achieving their goals, objectives, and strategies — that they become blind to the needs of others. Self-focused leaders tend to invest all their available energy into motivating people, dreaming up incentives that will cause others to meet *the leader's goals.* They will tell you that this is demonstrating their ability to focus on the goal. In truth, they do this because they need to — selfish behavior does not inspire. In turn, this causes people to feel used, alienated, and ignored. Self-focused leaders send repeated signals to parceners that the needs of others are secondary to those of the leader. In this environment, employees become

If you want a quality, act as if you already had it.

WILLIAM JAMES

resentful, sensing that their relationship to their leader is merely functional, that they are viewed merely as the means of production.

The first priority of the Aquarian leader is to serve. The servant-leader knows that parceners yearn to be heard, to be engaged not in debate but in genuine dialogue — not mind to mind, but heart to heart — a dialogue that springs from a loving intent and thus inspires.

How do we do this? How does the Inspirational Leader inspire? Here is an example. Suppose that we ask an employee this question: "How can I serve and inspire you?" Note the language — we are asking questions, not prescribing plans or solutions; we are offering to serve, and we are making it clear that we mean to listen to, and then act on, the response, whatever it might be.

Perhaps the employee might respond, "I recently remarried, and my youngest daughter is making life very difficult for my new spouse. I am feeling sad about this, and I would dearly love to heal this relationship. This is what would truly inspire me."

Note that although the conditions that lead to inspiration may be work-related, very often, they are not.

As a servant-leader, we might respond to this employee in this way, "We are a very well connected organization in our community. We know people who are professionals in this field, and if you would agree to it, I will make arrangements for you to find a professional of your choice, who will work with you to help heal this relationship. We will help to pay for the service and arrange your work schedule so that you can invest the time required."

Suppose that in time the relationship improves, even heals, isn't it entirely likely that an emotional and spiritual burden will be lifted from this employee, which in turn will transform their attitude, leading to improved productivity, increased loyalty, and greater effectiveness? Healing this broken relationship would enable this employee to shed the distraction of it, and thus divert the consuming negative energy into a greater commitment to the Cause of the leader and the organization.

Old story leaders will view such an approach with discomfort, believing this sounds more like therapy than leadership. But in the evolved organization, the role of the leader *is* to engage with people where it is important to *them* — to serve them. The servant-leader, and especially the Inspirational Leader, *is* therapist, mentor, teacher, guide, friend, role-model, and counselor all rolled into one. The role of the leader is not just to perform and represent functions, merely relating with other functions, but to remove the mask, to be a *real* human being who *relates* with other human beings at a level that really matters.

Most of us have no formal training in this area and shrink from such a role, from becoming "personal." Yet it is this level of engagement that inspires, and therefore as leaders we have no choice — we must learn to focus on the needs of others because it is in everyone's interest. We must become involved in what has traditionally become an "out-of-bounds" domain: the personal life of employees. In our hearts, we know this truth: a spouse who lives in an abusive relationship at home converts the abuse into dysfunctional behavior and brings it to work. This is costly, firstly to the organization because it reduces the effectiveness of the employee, and secondly to the human spirit because it is diminished. Our job as leaders is to do everything we can to inspire effectiveness *and* the human spirit. One doesn't need to be a rocket scientist to realize that an employee struggling with a chemical dependency or domestic violence is, firstly, experiencing great spiritual and physical pain, which we have a responsibility to help relieve if we can, and secondly, will not reach their full potential as a team member or parcener until these conditions improve. The Inspirational Leader does not shrink from involvement with the messy, but real, issues of peoples' lives, no matter what the risks or barriers may be, if it will inspire a soul and therefore inspire the team and the leader.

Caroline Martin and her husband own a successful lumber company, yet she has dedicated the last twenty-five years of her working life to healthcare. During that time, she has championed many difficult issues, overcome political and bureaucratic hurdles, introduced numerous breakthrough initiatives and currently leads the Riverside Health System team as Executive Director. Many people offer the tired cliché about loving their work so much they would pay to do it — but Caroline means it:

> It's not just being able to communicate clearly what the Cause is. It is equally important that I know what those on my team need, what the required resources are in order for them to contribute to that Cause, and how to operationalize an idea; to not give up when the money grows tight, the distractions grow great, and the enthusiasm wanes. I am blessed because I can share that joy with members on my team; we share reading materials, and discussions about those issues. I am blessed because I get paid to do what I would willingly pay to be a part of. I feel blessed every day. I don't know what's going to happen each day, but I know it's going to be exciting and good.

The spirit that energizes Caroline as a leader can be seen clearly shining through those words. Her parceners bask in this light and reflect it back to her. Perhaps the most accurate assessment of these qualities comes from parceners. Tracee Cameron, Director of Health Communications at Riverside, has worked with Caroline Martin for eleven years:

> Clearly the Inspirational Leadership comes from Caroline's desire to improve the health of our community ... and maybe the world. She thinks outside the box, away from the traditional financial reimbursement barriers, which could block our ability to accomplish health improvement. In all the years I've known Caroline, she has never vacillated from her vision.

> Caroline is a loving person; she freely expresses her love. She makes you feel like you are an important friend. She writes wonderful notes with loving messages; I keep her notes and occasionally reread them. What inspires me most are Caroline's Cause and her respect for those that work for her.

> Caroline's ideas about wellness are so full, robust, clear, and forceful; a person is immediately attracted to her beliefs and visions. I certainly am. She inspires me to make the Cause of wellness (a cure for sickness or the maximization of health) work. She often lets me know that I am a person who can make "wellness" happen. She freely gives me credit for my contributions. She focuses on your strengths, and minimizes your weaknesses or "human-ness."

> My perception of Caroline's bosses is that they are the typical Piscean leaders; our organization is very Piscean ... very bottom-line-driven and comfortable using motivational styles to influence change. Consequently, Caroline has to thrive with the realities of bottom-line-oriented, healthcare business while creating an environment, providing resources, and assembling a team to accomplish the ideal of improving health for people in our community.

Wouldn't any of us, having created an inspirational environment for others, be inspired if these words were used by parceners to describe us?

Says Caroline Martin, "I have been told by people who work on my team, that I believed in their capabilities before they did." That is the gift of the Inspirational Leader.

Courage under Fire

Ernest Hemingway defined grace as "courage under fire." Parceners learn as much, often more, about their leaders from what they *do*, rather than what they say. When leaders are under pressure or operating in unfamiliar conditions, parceners watch their reactions with a heightened sensitivity, searching for displays of grace — courage under fire. In these situations, they look to leaders for clear signals about their inner qualities, about whether he or she is a true Inspirational Leader. They learn in these circumstances about the leader's values and inner guide and use what they see to shape their assessment of how the leader might act with them in the future. Such events, of varying magnitude, occur each day, and each of them is a test of grace. Shortly after David Page became CEO at Fairview Health Systems, he received such a test:

> On the way to work, on the freeway just two miles from the hospital, one of our employees ran out of gas. Using her cell phone, she called her unit to let them know she would be late. Another employee offered to pick her up and put gas in her car. The driver of the stalled car got out when her colleague arrived with the gas. Meanwhile, two speeding cars approached — one a drug suspect and the other a police patrol car in pursuit. The cruiser crashed into the stalled car, killing our employee outright. The other employee was seriously injured and rushed to our hospital. She survived in the intensive care unit for several days until the decision was made to disconnect her life support system. Both of these people worked in the same unit, and their passing was a great shock. There were ceremonies, services, and heartfelt expressions of grief. Seven months later, I received a letter from the helper's family asking me why they were being sued by our hospital. The parents said, "We don't understand why you are suing us." They had already received a settlement, which they were using for a memorial to their daughter. I was horrified to learn that the family was being sued. They had gone through a terrible ordeal, were dealing with the tragedy, and now our organization appeared to be suing them to recover the signif-

icant shortfall, although the insurance company was actually suing on behalf of Fairview. I told the family that I would stop the litigation immediately and that they should not concern themselves with this matter further. I later learned that there was a shortfall between the cost of treatment and the amount insured and that my decision meant we would suffer a loss of $180,000, not easy when we are operating with some of the most challenging financial constraints in our history. But we just could not sue this family in their grief — they had just lost a child.

Such actions send powerful signals. David Page is a leader prepared to make decisions and assume the responsibility for them, based on right action. These are the acts of courage and grace that inspire parceners to inspire the leader.

The Setting for Inspiration: The Soulspace for Our Calling

Beauty is crucial to our well-being because it nourishes the soul. Without beauty, our soul withers, yet many of us immerse ourselves in ugliness every day. Even if we are fortunate enough to have found our Calling, we cannot inspire our souls if we practice it in hideous surroundings.

Visual aggression surrounds us, and it wears on the soul. The daily assaults made on our senses by self-centered commercialism, violence, and ugliness first penetrates our personalities, distressing our emotional selves, and then seeps into our soul, where it has the same effect. Some of the efficient and economical but ugly buildings in which people find themselves working are a case in point. But we can achieve efficiency and economy just as well through the opposites: service, love, and beauty. Indeed, we might ask ourselves what could be achieved through self-centered commercialism, violence, and ugliness that cannot be better achieved through service, love, and beauty? The former may take us to our short-term, personal goals, but the latter may do so, too, while, more importantly, at the same time rewarding our souls.

Nor is the mundane, the boring, the conventional or the cheapest, necessarily the most effective form of physical space. Many leaders are realizing that our physical environment, our Soulspace, must be more than functional; it must be fun, playful and entertaining, with textures, sounds, colors and smells that charm the senses, entrance the emotions, and speak to the soul. It must resemble life as it is richly lived, connecting us with the reality of human relationships and our yearning for community.

A visitor to the head office of British Airways, five miles west of London's Heathrow airport, is greeted by receptionists who flank the lobby as if they were checking you onto a flight, before passing between two giant wheels from the undercarriage of a jumbo jet. A corridor designed as a street, complete with cobblestones and sidewalk trees, links six small office blocks within the complex. The center of the complex mimics an English village square. Employees emerging from the basement car park cross the village square, as they would in a real village community, greeting and chatting with neighbors along the way. Employees are no longer tethered to their desks by telephone cords — having been liberated by digital wireless phones that double as their desk phone and can be carried anywhere. Employees can even order groceries on-line from a local supermarket and have them delivered to their cars before their daily commute. Such care and attention nurtures the soul. Canada's Nortel Networks has followed a similar pattern, having retrofitted a former factory into its head office, replete with streets, cafés, restaurants, indoor parks, and even a Zen garden.

Mark Scott, the Inspirational Leader and CEO of Mid-Columbia Medical Center in The Dalles, Oregon, describes the critical role of a Soulspace in the healing process in healthcare:

> The arts play a very important part in the healing process. There's no question that we have grown immune to such things as music, relaxation, massage therapy, artwork, story-telling and videos. These are all critical factors in creating an environment that encourages patient recovery and wellness. Our patient rooms are healing environments, and they are sacred healing spaces for us. Our hallways are elegant — they are frequently straightened up, nothing is ever allowed to litter the hallways. This is where most of our patients experience their first freedom of leaving the bed, therefore our hallways should not be cluttered with IV stands, laundry bags, trash bags, wheelchairs, dietary carts, pharmacy carts, etc. In healthcare we need to concentrate on maintaining our environments as sacred healing spaces if we expect to fully reach the inner souls of our patients and our staff in order to accelerate the pace of healing. The physical environment can enhance the well-being of both patients and staff. The focus is not just to make our

healthcare institutions nicer, prettier, and less institutional looking, but to acknowledge that the physical environment must change in order to enable a change in philosophy, to encourage a values-centered approach, and inculcate behavior changes that lead to patient-centered, humanistic care. We need to be aware of the real and symbolic messages of our environment. We must give the message to our patients that this is a caring, safe place; that "you are important here." We want patients to get well and stay well. We want them to know they are part of this community, that we encourage their mobility. We believe that art and beauty have important healing qualities.

Mark Scott describes an incident in which the creation of a Soulspace was crucial to the graceful passing of a patient, the healing of family members and the inspiration of staff:

I received a five-page letter from a lady in West Virginia about the passing of her mom in our hospital. She wrote: "My sister and I knew our mom was dying from toxic, lethal cancer. My sister called me and told me that mom had been readmitted and the physician said she had about twenty-four hours to live. It actually took her five days to pass away. It took us twenty-four hours to get from West Virginia to Oregon. We went to the patient activity room, which was elegant. There are quiet places, large screen TVs, salt-water fish tanks, nice sofas, and an area that overlooks the atrium where live entertainment occurs, a two-story waterfall, and a grand piano that people play." This letter was about how these two daughters took their mom to her room. They laughed, cried, reminisced. They could hear a nurse playing a piano elsewhere, and their mom listened. They asked the primary care nurse if they could take their mom to where the piano was, and the nurse stayed and played for them, accepting specific requests from their mom.

Our hospital has a kitchen with a small dining room in which family members can cook meals that are within dietary restrictions. The next day, they cooked a full Thanksgiving dinner. They knew that their mom was too sick to eat it, but they knew that what was more important were the smells, the stories, and the love. The next day, they baked Christmas cookies and sang carols. The two daughters knew why their mom was passing away because they were frequently shown her chart, and this helped them to understand and come to terms with her passing. The sisters celebrated their mom's passing with grace and thanks in a Soulspace. That's healing.

Doug Upchurch, former Executive Director of the Information Technology Training Association, says, "In our office space, we have two special rooms. We have a kids' room — this is for sick kids. Nannies can come in with them. It is not uncommon to have kids here during the week. There is a place for them to hang out. We also have a choir room. We call this the place to go where our souls can sing. We believe that we need to have an employee area. This includes natural beauty, music, and candles. We believe that this should be a wonderful relaxing place. These are fun things that we are doing."

Over the years, my own organization has evolved in a similar way. Our offices are located in a log house, perched at the edge of a cliff overlooking a seven-hundred-acre wilderness that unfolds into the valley four hundred feet below. The offices are wrapped in six-by-eight-foot windows that enable colleagues and visitors to connect with the spectacular views, which change with each magical season and weather pattern.

I have a great deal of company in the house, especially in the morning when nobody calls.

HENRY DAVID
THOREAU

The panorama is breathtaking and the silence extraordinary. Visitors arriving for the first time are astounded by the awe-inspiring views; even regular visitors return to their favorite spot to stand and gaze for a few moments to enjoy the pristine tranquility before settling into the business that brought them to our Soulspace. Hummingbirds feed near all of the office windows during the summer, and songbirds visit the many feeders placed strategically for everyone to enjoy. Deer often cross the property pausing to watch us as we watch them. In the native tradition, the deer is the symbol of gentleness, reminding us that we have created a gentle environment and our intent to be gentle with each other. Skiing is five minutes away, a swimming pool beckons outside, and trails through the woods offer opportunities for exercise, reflection, and conversation.

Each week, we hold a Wisdom Circle in the main office, warmed by the airtight stove in the colder months, and in the warmer times, we gather at the end of the thirty-foot cantilevered deck that thrusts out over the cliff edge. Any team member may read an inspiring poem, quote, or essay to precede and end each meeting. Breaking bread together is an important ritual for our team. Those members who are not traveling bring the components of lunch and prepare it together in the kitchen, which is fully stocked with refreshments and snacks. Team members frequently bring treats to share: homemade cookies, cakes, soups, even wine. On one occasion, we made grape jelly together from wild grapes collected from the local area, turning the event into a collaborative project. We have a surround-sound stereo system with hundreds of CDs and a library with several thousand books. Jasmine, the second daughter of my assistant, spent the first eighteen months of her life coming to our offices every day, where we would vie for the opportunity to carry her around while talking on our portable phones. Although Jasmine now attends daycare, we still have Spirit the wonder dog, to entertain us each day! Though we may be pastoral and romantic, cutting-edge technology connects our global team of Associates, hundreds of members of The Higher Ground Community, and our clients and suppliers.

You may be reading this and thinking, "This guy isn't in the real world. He should come and smell the coffee and see the awful place where I work." But you and I are the same — we have choices. I have always wanted to work with inspired teams, and I've always known this is not possible in uninspiring physical environments. Consequently, I have always refused to pay rents to landlords for efficient but ugly buildings. Even in my former life thirty years ago, when we founded the head offices of Manpower Limited, we refused to locate in the city, choosing instead a rural town that offered convenient commuting for our team members.

A soft smooth, slippery thing and therefore of a nature which easily slips in and permeates our souls. For I affirm that the good is the beautiful.

PLATO

We were one of the first companies to hire an architect to design office landscaping; we were one of Herman Miller's first customers, outfitting our entire offices with modular, custom-designed, and personally chosen furniture. We built a meditation room, we abandoned dress codes, installed kitchens, loaded the health, insurance, disability, and retirement plans — in short, we went out of our way to create a Soulspace for our team. We wanted to create the conditions in which they would be inspired, and in turn inspire us. We wanted to be Inspirational Leaders — we all have the choice.

Our physical workspace must connect us with Nature — we cannot attain extraordinary levels of achievement when we are disconnected from the Earth. Our association with the Earth is not only natural, but also vital to our souls. The Earth represents our very physical essence: we are made of earth and, ultimately, we are returned to earth. For reasons that are not always obvious therefore, we all experience a connection with landscape and the natural world. A numinous voice calls to us from the rocks and streams, from the birds and fishes, from the stars and storms. A mystical beauty speaks to our souls, reminding us where we belong and that we share the life force of the Universe. Anyone who has spoken to a rock knows that this is true. Plastic plants and fake trees are no substitute for the real thing. If we are surrounded by plastic and fakery, our thoughts will become the same.

If you work in a dismal environment, ask yourself what is holding you back from changing it, making it better, converting it into a Soulspace. In addition to tradition and inertia, what *real* reasons are in your way? If you love the people you work with and you want to inspire them — why aren't you spoiling them, making them feel special, and indulging their needs?

There are only two ways of spreading light — to be the candle or the mirror that reflects it.

EDITH WHARTON

Christopher Morley wrote, "Truth is the strong compost in which beauty may sometimes germinate." Perhaps it is also the other way around: beauty is the compost, which may sometimes germinate truth. Who can nurture the urge to violence or mendacity when beauty and love are cradling them? What matters to Inspirational Leaders is that they meet the needs of all the members of the team sharing the Soulspace, whether they are on the payroll or are partners, suppliers, and customers. Inspirational Leaders want them all to be inspired to produce the finest work in their field. A Soulspace, the physical beauty with which we surround ourselves at work, is essential for our inspiration. Beauty is holiness. Beauty is grace. Beauty is sacred. As Josiah Gilbert Holland said, "The soul, like the body, lives by what it feeds on."

Outing the Closet Human

The ego is like the moon. Though it can be bright at times, and often full, it always depends on the sun for its light. It, like the ego, has a shadow side, which will remain dark as long as it is not exposed to the warmth and light of the sun. The soul is like the sun. It is the source of its own energy and light. It shines its light freely and consistently. It shares and warms. It heals and nourishes. It even adds light to the ego-moon, which otherwise would be permanently cold and dark. By turning our egos to the warmth and light of the soul and inviting its healing and loving power, we will grow and be bright and warm.

At work, our souls tend to be in the shadow of our personalities because we think of each other as "functions" (executive, teacher, parent, pilot, physician, letter carrier), instead of what we really are: spiritual beings enjoying an earthly experience. We wear an ego mask, pretending that we are strong, potent, invulnerable heroes and, at work in particular, we often labor under the delusion that it is unseemly to permit our feelings to infuse our decisions.

But this is not real life — it is a lie. We become masks locked in arid conversations with other masks. And when we behave like this we are *closet humans.*

We need to "come out," to own up to being human, to being vulnerable and fragile, to owning pain, needing love, compassion, and forgiveness, to wanting more from life than profit improvement, a paycheck, or a promotion. In short, we need to come out by declaring ourselves to be *real* humans. We need to conduct communications with each other that are authentic, truthful, and deep, instead of pretending to be the fictitious macho characters we have taught our personalities to idolize. We need to discuss matters that serve a higher purpose *as well* as the data, the metrics, the tasks at hand, and the bottom line, because if we limit our dialogue to the secular and the material, our relationships will be brittle and barren. We need to reveal ourselves to each other for what we really are — spiritual beings enjoying a human experience, whole people who are parents, spouses, lovers, teachers, and learners, who laugh and cry, hurt and heal, but above all have loving intent and are here to serve each other.

When we come out, by revealing our true emotional and spiritual selves, a remarkable thing will happen. For the first time, our masks will fall, and others will recognize us for who we truly are. As a result, they in turn will be emboldened to reveal their humanness with us, and we will come to know each other for the first time. Others will join with us and thus create the beginnings of a Sanctuary — my definition for a state of mind among people who share values. In time, others will notice the extraordinary sense of teamwork and the personal effectiveness and energy flowing from this Sanctuary. They will be drawn to it and they will want to join. Others will want to come out, too, and some will want to form their own Sanctuaries. This spontaneous rejuvenation of authenticity works like an immune system that has been spurred into new vigor. Sanctuaries will sprout in disparate parts of the organization, replacing the toxic relationships that existed before and healing the souls trapped within corporate walls. This magic produces a bonus — because organizations are simply collections of individual spirits, when these spirits heal one at a time, the sum of them eventually heals, too. The result is in greater organizational effectiveness and performance — an organization of inspired souls. Then, as leaders, we will become inspired.

Old story leaders are the last to emerge from the closet because misinformation about leadership styles is most widespread among them. My experience in working with great organizations and their leaders is that eventually they become keen to capitalize (literally) on the great spiritual renaissance that is underway in our society — *when they finally recognize it*. Enlightened leaders are keen to grasp this new opportunity, either because they know a bandwagon when they see one, or because they have genuinely come to realize that people really are an organization's most important asset. It doesn't much matter which — the organizational missionaries we call Inspirational Leaders take their successes any way they can get them.

This is the way of the enlightened changemaker, the Inspirational Leader. Demanding change from others seldom works. We want the keys to the kingdom, but the more we demand that the King should hand them over, the more we will be resisted. Gandhi had a better idea: "You must be the change you wish to see in the world."

We get commitment by making a commitment.

The greatest leaders in history whom we each now revere most dearly are the ones that continue to inspire us most. The leaders that we each know and love at a personal level today are also the ones who inspire us the most. Inspirational Leaders inspire us for one reason only: they love us. Inspirational Leaders have a love affair with parceners; an intense affair of the heart, and this is what fuels their capacity for inspiring others. Inspiration can only come from love — it cannot come from any other place. Every Inspirational Leader makes a soul connection with parceners at a level that captivates us both — leader and parcener.

Inspirational Leadership® is love made visible.

In a Nutshell: The Seven Key Questions

The Inspirational Leader asks seven key questions and then dedicates their life's work to finding the answers. They are:

- What is my Destiny?
- What is my Cause?
- What is my Calling?
- Is my Calling aligned with my Cause?
- How may I serve those whom I lead?
- How can I guide the contribution of brilliance from those I lead?
- Am I inspiring others in everything I say and do?

Inspiring others is an act of service that flows from love. Motivational leaders love others, of course, but they love themselves most; Inspirational Leaders love themselves, too, but they love others more. Parceners read the difference in a heartbeat. They sense the presence of a motivator: to them, the manipulative and self-focused agendas of the motivational leader are often so transparent. So is the commitment to ego and personality, to the superficial and to the material. Inspirational Leaders love others so genuinely they cannot resist serving them — and parceners are at once inspired by this congruence. The result is a connection of souls, of people doing soulwork, and of the creation of a Sanctuary. These are magical moments and magical places in which to work because Inspirational Leaders are *fully present*. In these exhilarating states, we become inspired. And to the great joy of those around us, we are inspired to offer our greatest gifts — we are called to release the music within us.

BLESSING FOR AN INSPIRATIONAL LEADER

Thank you for being clear about your Destiny
And following your Calling.
Thank you for being a caring Listener,
For inviting me to bare my Soul and share my dreams with you,
And for hearing my story and asking about the path that I am on;
For being interested in my LIFE as well as my work.
Thank you for not wearing a mask, for being a Real human,
And revealing the genuine article, when I ask;
For being vulnerable, not invincible,
For owning your fears and learning about mine.
Thank you for understanding the difference between

motivation and Inspiration
And for knowing the right time and place for each one.
Thank you for being a Mentor, generously sharing your
wisdom with me,
Including the little secrets and special tricks that really
make a difference.
I pay tribute to your courageous heart that so invigorates
you and others,
Causing you to keep trying even when the world has no ears for you;
Lesser beings would have given up long ago.
I recognize you for telling the truth and keeping your promises —
I offer you, in return, my complete trust and loyalty.
Thank you for having faith in me, patiently encouraging my potential,
And helping me to discover my greatness.
Thank you for running interference through the "system"
on my behalf,
Promoting my cause, being fair and even-handed and
defending me when appropriate.
Thank you for having vision, always seeing the bigger picture,
Dreaming in Technicolor while others settle for a world of gray.
Thank you for getting out of my way and encouraging me to do my job
So that we can both excel at what we each do best.
I celebrate your Creativity, the muse within you who asks "Why"
And the divine being within you who thinks more about
solutions than problems.
I admire your Grace, your peaceful intent, your search for
balance and friendship and
The way you calm disagreements,
Always focusing on what unites us, not what divides us,
Playing to Strengths, not weaknesses.
Thank you for Growing and encouraging me to do the same.
Thank you for Serving, for putting me first and yourself next.
I honor you for balancing the energies of your Personality
with those of your Soul,
Always considering both — in yourself and others.
Thank you for being a beautiful leader, for loving me and
others and yourself.

Suggested Bibliography

I am often asked what I am currently reading. This is a list, in no particular order, of books that have recently inspired or informed me. Some are old, some are new, but all have been a treat for my Soul — and I hope they will inspire yours.

1. *Anatomy of the Spirit: The Seven Stages of Power and Healing*, by Caroline Myss (Random House/Value Publishing, 1977). A brilliant review of energy medicine and spiritual healing.

2. *Sacred Hoops: Spiritual Lessons of a Hardwood Warrior*, by Phil Jackson (Hyperion, 1995). Small but potent book by the legendary coach of the Chicago Bulls, describing his relationship with Michael Jordan and how he used Christian and Native American wisdom to lead the best team in the NBA.

3. *A Return to Love: Reflections on the Principles of A Course in Miracles*, by Marianne Williamson (HarperCollins, 1992). "A spiritual travel guide for our journey back to the truth we were born with"; beautifully written and underscoring the importance of love in our lives.

4. *The Reinvention of Work: A New Vision of Livelihood for Our Time*, by Matthew Fox (HarperCollins, 1994). Former Dominican priest, defrocked by the Pope for his radical and outspoken views, writes beautifully about why work isn't working and what to do about it. Check out his other works, too, especially *Creation Spirituality*.

5. *The Heart Aroused: Poetry and Preservation of the Soul in Corporate America*, by David Whyte (Currency Doubleday, 1994). Welsh-American living in Seattle, writing lyrically about work and leadership, using stories, metaphors, and his own poetry, as well as that of others.

6. *Buddhism, The Religion of No-Religion: The Edited Transcripts*, by Alan Watts (Tuttle, 1996). Alan Watts' lectures on Buddhist thought, including Zen and the Tibetan Tradition, delivered in 1965 and 1969 and transcribed by his son.

7. *Nourishing the Soul: Discovering the Sacred in Every Day Life*, edited by Anne Simpkinson, Charles Simpkinson and Rose Solari (HarperCollins, 1995). Eclectic collection of essays by Thomas Moore, Clarissa Pinkola Estes, Robert A. Johnson, Jack Cornfield, Deena Metzger, and others.

8. *Stories of the Spirit, Stories of the Heart: Parables of the Spiritual Path from Around the World*, edited by Christina Feldman and Jack Kornfield (HarperSanFrancisco, 1991). Teaching stories handed down over time by

the great masters, including Jesus, Buddha, and Ramakrishna and many of the great wisdom traditions, including Sufi, Zen, Buddhism, Christianity, and Islam.

9. *The Soul of the Firm,* by C. William Pollard (Harper Business, 1996). The chairman of The ServiceMaster Company describes this remarkable organization and how its values have created a business that honors and serves people and, as a result, makes tons of money.

10. *The Fisher King and the Handless Maiden: Understanding the Wounded Feeling Function in Masculine and Feminine Psychology,* by Robert A. Johnson (HarperSanFrancisco, 1993). Two traditional fables unlocked and reinterpreted using Jungian psychology and metaphor.

11. *It's Easier Than You Think: The Buddhist Way to Happiness,* by Sylvia Boorstein (HarperCollins, 1995). Slim volume by a beloved Buddhist teacher, who makes traditional Buddhist teaching understandable for the beginner and for the seeker; entertaining and filled with charm and warmth.

12. *The Soul's Code: In Search of Character and Calling,* by James Hillman (Random House, 1996). A wonderful and original insight into the subject of Calling and Destiny. Hillman describes his "acorn theory," in which he suggests that "each life is formed by a particular image, an image that is the essence of that life and calls it to a destiny, just as the mighty oak's destiny is written in the tiny acorn."

13. *The Wisdom of Baltasar Gracian: A Practical Manual for Good and Perilous Times,* adapted by J. Leonard Kaye (Pocket Books, 1992). Baltasar Gracian was a Jesuit priest who counseled kings and was the genius of his age three hundred years ago. Intimidated by Gracian's wisdom and genius, his bishop harassed him, confiscated his manuscripts, and spent years trying to silence him. The enduring quality of Gracian's work is a testimony to the indomitable spirit of humans and the love that can still reside in the heart despite the ridicule and torment of others.

14. *The Cancer Battle Plan: Six Strategies for Beating Cancer from a Recovered "Hopeless Case,"* by Anne E. Frahm with David J. Frahm (Pinon Press, 1994). When my son-in-law was diagnosed with leukemia and given sixty days to live, like others before me, I immediately devoured every book I could find on the subject. My agent and his wife, Ron and Denise Szymanski, sent me this remarkable story of a woman who successfully overcame breast cancer. She first describes how she did it, and then tells the story of how she turned this experience into a teaching organization for others. It is a wonderful, practical, and hopeful recovery manual for those who may die unless they quickly discover the keys to living.

15. *The Nordstrom Way: Inside America's #1 Customer Service Company,* by Robert Spector and Patrick McCarthy (John Wiley, 1995) and *Nuts: Southwest Airlines' Crazy Recipe for Business and Personal Success,* by Kevin and Jackie Frieberg (Bard Press, 1996). Neither of these books will win a prize for great literature, but they tell the stories of Nordstrom and Southwest Airlines respectively — two organizations setting the standards for "new paradigm leadership" in the workplace.

16. *Jamming: The Art and Discipline of Business Creativity,* by John Kao (Harper Business, 1996). Twenty years ago, John Kao and about three other people, including myself, were the only people teaching "Entrepreneurship" in North America at the graduate school level. We learned from each other as pioneers and windmill-tilters. John is also a gifted jazz pianist. Over the last two decades, he has developed his knowledge of entrepreneurship, which he taught at Harvard, to an inclusive expertise in Creativity. Combining his musical gifts and his teaching skills, he has written an excellent book about Creativity that uses the jazz jam session as a brilliant metaphor.

17. *The Seven Spiritual Laws of Success: A Practical Guide to the Fulfillment of Your Dreams,* by Deepak Chopra (New World Library, 1994). Anything Deepak Chopra writes is interesting and thoughtful. This little book is potent because it contains a complete template for living a happy life — no modest achievement. It is well written and a beautiful map for a life of spirit.

18. *Business as a Calling: Work and the Examined Life,* by Michael Novak (Free Press, 1996). After studying for the priesthood for twelve years, and six months before becoming ordained, the author abandoned his studies to become a theologian and writer. He has been a U.S. ambassador, and author of twenty-five books. He always writes thoughtful, provocative material about spirituality and values, and this book is no exception. A fabulous view of work as a spiritual Calling and commerce as a potentially unifying, peace-giving and loving activity for humans on this planet. A rousing pick-me-up if your spirits ever flag or your faith in the system ever sags.

19. *Reflections on Leadership: How Robert K. Greenleaf's Theory of Servant-Leadership Influenced Today's Top Management Thinkers,* edited by Larry C. Spears (Executive Director of The Greenleaf Center for Servant-Leadership) (John Wiley, 1995). Robert Greenleaf worked for thirty-eight years for AT&T as Director of Management Research. During those years and his twelve retirement years (he died in 1990), he developed his theories of "Servant-leadership," which are a way of life for those today who aspire to lead with spirit, values, and love. Larry Spears has pulled together a marvelous collection of essays by such writers, practitioners and consultants as Scott Peck, Peter Senge, Max DuPree, Ron Zemke, and others who

describe the major impact of Greenleaf's work on their lives and the think-ing of today's evolved leaders.

20. *Molecules of Emotion: Why You Feel the Way You Feel*, by Candace B. Pert (Scribner, 1997). I have followed Candace Pert's work for years. She is one of the world's leading neuroscientists and made some of the earliest discoveries of neuropeptides. One of my presentations, "The Hand or the Fist," and the chapter entitled "The Alchemy of the Soul" in *Reclaiming Higher Ground*, as well as my audiotape for healing migraines called "The Healer Within," draws very heavily on her work. This is a brilliant book that begins to make the links between emotions, mind, spirit, and neuro-chemistry.

21. *The Prophet's Way: Touching the Power of Life*, by Thom Hartmann (Mythic Books, 1997). This is a marvelous, true-life spiritual adventure story by a gifted spiritual leader and exemplar. Hartmann shows what it takes to be connected to our inner divinity and how we have lost our connection to "the heartbeat of the world."

22. *Entering the Circle: Ancient Secrets of Siberian Wisdom Discovered by a Russian Psychiatrist*, by Olga Kharitidi (HarperSanFrancisco, 1996). This is a remarkable true-life autobiography of a Soviet psychiatrist who encounters a shaman and witnesses real shamanic healing. This experience changes her life and therefore the way she practices medicine. Because of her shamanic experiences she is unable to practice medicine in the old ways she has relied on. She begins to heal psychiatric patients who have been locked up for years in a depressing psychiatric ward of a gulag hospital, healing instantly patients who had been deemed incurable for years, and she is unable to explain her new "miraculous" powers. This creates conflict between the old traditions and the new — the same conflicts we experience between the "old paradigm" management theories and the new paradigm concepts based on spirit and values at work. An excellent metaphor for the two solitudes of current leadership theory.

23. *Emissary of Light: Adventures with the Secret Peacemakers*, by James F. Twyman (Aslan Publishing, 1996). Story about a musician and teacher of "A Course in Miracles" who wrote twelve peace songs based on the peace prayers of the twelve major world religions. He embarks on an incredible journey to the world's most violent war zone to sing and pray for peace and, while there, encounters a mythical community invoking the greatest spiritual power in the world's area of greatest bloodshed and conflict. Inspiring.

24. *Open Heart, Clear Mind*, by Thubten Chodron (Snow Lion Publications, 1990). This is an easy-to-read explanation of Buddhist philosophy.

25. ***Zen Keys: A Guide to Zen Practice***, by Thich Nhat Hanh (Doubleday, 1995). Perhaps the most gifted and beloved thinker and writer in Zen Buddhism and tireless advocate for peace practicing in the West today. Originally written in 1974, and completely updated in this edition, this book by the great Zen Master provides a fresh perspective on Zen Buddhism for Westerners suffering from hurry-sickness.

26. ***The Book of Life: Daily Meditations with Krishnamurti***, by J. Krishnamurti (HarperSanFrancisco, 1995). The writings of an extraordinary sage of our time, J. Krishnamurti, arranged into 365 daily meditations, developed thematically over seven days, illuminating the concepts of freedom, personal transformation, living fully awake and life.

27. ***Your Life Is Your Message*** (1992) and ***Take Your Time*** (1994) (Hyperion), both by Eknath Easwaran. I had not heard of this author before. He is the Founder and Director of the Blue Mountain Center for meditation in Tomales, California. Both are thoughtful little books that offer guidance to balancing our lives.

28. ***Daybreak: 52 Things Nature Teaches Us***, by Amy E. Dean (M. Evans and Company, 1996). This book is a collection of essays that link the natural world with our daily material reality and paint a metaphor from which we can learn. For instance, communications are explained with the metaphor of African vervet monkeys; toads help to explain individuality; and ravens demonstrate problem solving. Loaded with wonderful quotations and twenty-two black-and-white photographs from the American Museum of Natural History.

29. ***Where Did the Money Go? A Beginner's Guide to Basic Business Scorekeeping***, by Ellen Rohr (ISBN number 0-9665719-0-8; http://www.amazon.com/exec/obidos/tg/detail/-/0966571924/103-3435867-72862672?vi= glance). A book about business BASICS, the stuff you wish someone had explained to you long ago about confusing business and accounting terms. After this, you'll know what your banker and accountant are talking about. It will teach you how to keep track of the money, so you can make more of it ... to share, to contribute, to grow, to energize ... to use to make the world a better place.

30. ***The Diving Bell and the Butterfly,*** by Jean-Dominique Bauby (Knopf, 1997). This is a wonderful little memoir (132 pages) written by the author, the former editor-in-chief of the French edition of *Elle* magazine in Paris, who at age forty-three suffered a massive stroke that left him totally paralyzed and able to use only his left eyelid. Once witty and gregarious, he is now imprisoned, but his spirit will not die — so he writes a poetic, ironic, touching and whimsical book about his experiences by dictating to a friend through the use of his eyelid! The book was published two days before he died in 1996 and became a number one bestseller across Europe.

31. *Spiritual Literacy: Reading the Sacred in Everyday Life,* by Frederic and Mary Ann Brussatt (Scribner, 1996). I have been reading this book consistently for ages because it is such a gift. It is a 608-page spiritual banquet containing 650 wonderful anecdotes, stories, poems, homilies, and advice. Curl up beside a fire and bury yourself in this beauty, and I bet it will be hard to pull you away! Using a very creative format, the Brussatts have created an Alphabet of Spiritual Literacy — from Attention to Zeal — including spiritual perspectives on things, places, nature, animals, leisure, creativity, service, body, relationships, and community along the way.

32. *Rewiring the Corporate Brain: Using the New Science to Rethink How We Structure and Lead Organizations,* by Danah Zohar (Berret-Koehler, 1997). Today, anyone trying to unravel the mysteries of leadership must first understand the basic concepts behind quantum, chaos, and the latest brain science which is revolutionizing our thinking about the world and therefore leadership. This short book offers interesting models and cases while making the link between the new science and offering inspiring alternatives to traditional structures in corporate design, practice, and implementation. Danah Zohar has also written several other important works, including *The Quantum Self.*

33. *Stone Soup for the World: Life-changing Stories of Kindness & Courageous Acts of Service*, edited by Marianne Larned (Conari Press, 1998). A collection of inspiring stories of individuals who have made this world a better place through their personal passion and commitment to service, from the famous (Nelson Mandela, Martin Luther King, Mother Teresa, Bette Midler, Paul Newman) to scores of ordinary folk doing extraordinary things to build communities and make a difference. Contains details of how to find and contact most of the people described and how to join their cause.

34. *Illuminated Prayers,* by Marianne Williamson (Simon & Schuster, 1997). This is a beautifully produced work with delightful illustrations containing thoughtful and inspiring prayers and meditations for any occasion.

35. *Tuesdays with Morrie: An old Man, a Young Man, and Life's Greatest Lesson,* by Mitch Albom, (Doubleday, New York, 1997). Mitch rediscovers his old professor, Morrie, in the last weeks of his life. He accepts a final private "class" with Morrie, meeting every Tuesday to learn the lessons of life.

Endnotes

Introduction

1 Andy Grove and Bethany McLean, "Taking on Prostate Cancer," *Fortune*, May 13, 1996.

2 Mike Verespej, "It's Time to Find a Better Way," *Industry Week*, January 18, 1999, p. 14.

3 Pierre Teilhard de Chardin, *The Phenomenon of Man*, trans. Bernard Wall (New York: Harper & Row, 1959).

Chapter 1

4 Chris Argyris, "Empowerment: The Emperor's New Clothes," *Harvard Business Review*, May–June, 1998, pp. 98–105.

5 Nina Munk, "Finished at Forty," *Fortune*, February 1, 1999, p. 50.

6 Rita Koselka, "For Whom the Bell Tolls," *Forbes*, December 2, 1996, pp. 127–28.

7 "It's the Manager, Stupid," *The Economist*, August 8, 1998.

8 Lance H.K. Secretan, *Reclaiming Higher Ground: Creating Organizations that Inspire the Soul* (Alton: The Secretan Center Inc., 2003).

9 Lance H.K. Secretan, *The Way of the Tiger: Gentle Wisdom for Turbulent Times* (Alton: The Secretan Center Inc., 1990).

10 Gene Koretz, "How Many Hours in a Workweek?" *Business Week*, June 16, 1997, p. 12.

11 Michael A. Verespej, "Uninspiring Leadership," *Industry Week*, February 1, 1999, p. 11.

12 Anne Fisher, "The 100 Best Companies to Work for in America," *Fortune*, January 12, 1998, pp. 69–95.

13 Nancy J. Lyons, "Managing the Volunteer Workforce," *Inc.*, December, 1997, pp. 73–81.

14 David Menzies, "The Marketer as Helping Hand," *The Financial Post 500*, 1997.

15 Charles Fishman, "Making IT With the Golden Rule," *Financial Post*, February 17, 1999.

Chapter 2

16 Pierre Teilhard de Chardin, *The Phenomenon of Man*, trans. Bernard Wall (New York: Harper & Row, 1959).

17 Lisa Chadderdon, "Monkey See, Monkey Do," *Fast Company*, April 1999, p. 56.

18 Janice Maloney, "The Mighty Finn," *Time*, October 26, 1998, p. 69; Scott McCormack and Cecile Daurat, "Icons of the Net," *Forbes*, September 7, 1998, p. 216; "Revenge of the Hackers," *The Economist*, July 11, 1998, p. 63.

19 *New Age Journal*, January/February, 1997.

Chapter 3

20 Lance H.K. Secretan, *Managerial Moxie: The 8 Proven Steps to Empowering Your Employees and Supercharging your Company* (Toronto: Prima Publishing, 1993).

Chapter 4

21 Nina Munk, "My Life Is Miserable. You've Made a BIG Difference," *Forbes*, March 24, 1997, p. 40.

22 Jennifer Harrison and Rebecca Piirto Heath, "Advertising Joins the Journey of the Soul," *American Demographics*, vol. 9, no. 6, June 1997, p. 22(6).

Chapter 6

23 John P. Kotter, *Matsushita Leadership* (New York: Free Press, 1997).

24 Dawn Schauble, *Survey on Employment Benefit Preferences* (New York: William M. Mercer).

Chapter 7

25 Reprinted from *Touching Peace: Practicing the Art of Mindful Living* (1992) by Thich Nhat Hanh with permission of Parallax Press, Berkeley, California.

26 Leslie R. Crutchfield, "Teaching Jazz: Creating Community," in *Stone Soup for the World*, edited by Marianne Larned (Berkeley, CA: Conari Press, 1998), p. 21.

27 James Hillman, *The Soul's Code: In Search of Character and Calling* (New York: Random House, 1996), p. 8.

28 Ibid, p. 6.

29 *USA Today*, October, 1998.

Chapter 8
30 Eric Schine, "CalPERS Grand Inquisitor," *Business Week*, February 24, 1997.

31 Jeffrey Kluger, "The Suicide Seeds," *Time*, February 1, 1999, p. 43.

32 Lance H.K. Secretan, *Reclaiming Higher Ground: Creating Organizations that Inspire the Soul* (Alton: The Secretan Center Inc., 2003).

33 Ibid, p. 245.

Chapter 9
34 *Fortune*, February 17, 1997, p. 127.

35 Joel Stein, "Bosses from Hell," *Time*, December 7, 1998, p. 153.

36 Tim Stevens, "Chief Among US," *Industry Week*, November 16, 1998, p. 33.

37 Donald L. Bartlett and James B. Steele, "Fantasy Islands," *Time*, November 16, 1998, p. 68.

38 Keith H. Hammonds, "The Issue in the U.S. Is Employment, Not Employability," *Business Week*, June 17, 1996, pp. 72B-E.

39 William A. Knaus, Elizabeth A. Draper, Douglas P. Wagner, and Jack E. Zimmerman, "An Evaluation of Outcome from Intensive Care in Major Medical Centers," *Annals of Internal Medicine*, vol. 104 (1986), pp. 410–18.

40 Ann Marsh, "Slice of Life," *Forbes*, April 22, 1997, pp. 64–65.

41 "The Invitation" from *The Invitation* by Oriah Mountain Dreamer. Copyright © 1999 by Oriah Mountain Dreamer. Reprinted by permission of HarperCollins Publishers Inc.

Chapter 10
42 Thomas J. Peters and Robert H. Waterman, *In Search of Excellence: Lessons from America's Best-Run Companies* (New York: Harper & Row, 1982).

43 *Escape* by D. H. Lawrence, from the *Complete Poems of D. H. Lawrence* by D. H. Lawrence, edited by V. de Sola Pinto & F. W. Roberts. Copyright © 1964, 1971 by Angelo Ravagli and C. M. Weekley, Executors of the Estate of Frieda Lawrence Ravagli. Used by permission of Viking Penguin, a division of Penguin Putnam Inc.

Chapter 11
44 Lance H.K. Secretan, *The Way of the Tiger: Gentle Wisdom for Turbulent Times* (Toronto: The Secretan Center Inc., 1990).

45 Taylor Branch, *America in the King Years, 1963–1965* (New York: Simon and Schuster, 1999).

46 Ursula K. Le Guin, *Lao-Tzu, Tao Te Ching: A Book About the Way and the Power of the Way* (Boston: Shambhala, 1997).

47 Caroline Myss, *Anatomy of the Spirit: The Seven Stages of Power and Healing* (New York: Random House/Value Publishing, 1997).

Blueprint for New Leadership

Please sign and send to the address below or use the Internet form at
http://www.secretan.com/html/charter98.html

We invite all leaders to subscribe to these leadership ideals:

1) **The role of the organization:** We are agents of positive change.

2) **Purpose:** Our work inspires.

3) **Sacredness and respect:** We treat all beings as sacred.

4) **Honorable profits:** We earn honorable profits from life-affirming activities.

5) **Spirit at work:** Our work is our spiritual practice.

6) **Values:** Our values determine our strategy.

7) **Truth-telling:** We tell the truth and keep our promises.

8) **Servant-leadership:** Our Leaders serve.

9) **Fun:** Our work is fun.

10) **Love:** Love is the heart of our work.

11) **Learning:** Learning fuels our Souls.

12) **Change:** We start all change from within — one person at a time.

13) **Potential:** We create opportunities for individuals to realize their potential.

14) **Beauty:** We create beautiful surroundings that inspire the Soul.

15) **Balance:** We balance work with life.

16) **Authenticity:** We live and work authentically.

17) **Courage:** We are courageous.

18) **Grace:** We maintain a state of grace.

Blueprint for New Leadership describes the contemporary workplace for which people are yearning today.

We invite you to endorse this **Blueprint for New Leadership** by making yours one of a million signatures we anticipate receiving. Ask your friends and your work colleagues to add their names, too. This is an international plebiscite, designed to change the way leaders think about their followers at work. It is our hope that the **Blueprint for New Leadership** will inspire a new paradigm of leadership thinking, and become the guiding principles for effective, values-centered, spiritually guided organizations everywhere.

1. Signed by:

Name: _____

Organization:_____

Address:_____

_____

Phone: (   )_____

2. Signed by:

Name: _____

Organization:_____

Address:_____

_____

Phone: (   )_____

The Secretan Center Inc. R.R. #2, Alton, ON, L0N 1A0, CANADA
e-mail: info@secretan.com; World Wide Web: http://www.secretan.com

Index